VOCABULARY 1000

VOCABULARY 1000

MORTON J. CRONIN
CALIFORNIA STATE COLLEGE
at Los Angeles

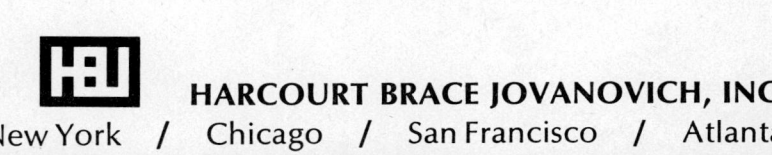
HARCOURT BRACE JOVANOVICH, INC.
New York / Chicago / San Francisco / Atlanta

© 1969 by Harcourt Brace Jovanovich, Inc.

All rights reserved. No part of this publication may be reproduced or transmitted in any form or by any means, electronic or mechanical, including photocopy, recording, or any information storage and retrieval system, without permission in writing from the publisher.

ISBN: 0-15-594985-3

Library of Congress Catalog Card Number: 72-78821

Printed in the United States of America

Preface

Vocabulary 1000 is a programed book with three objectives: to induce the student to take a friendly interest in words; to teach him prefixes, roots, and suffixes, thereby strengthening his understanding of familiar words and providing him with clues to the meaning of unfamiliar words; and to add new words to his vocabulary.

The book is of modest length, for its aim is to whet the student's appetite for words, not to flood him with new vocabulary. In particular, it avoids lists of words. The exercises move briskly, but they present one word at a time. They build from familiar words to more difficult ones, giving the student confidence by showing him that he knows more than he realizes, improving his grip on words he has already encountered, and providing analogies that will help him learn new words. And the book sustains the student's interest by taking up a different word in each frame and immediately requiring that he do something with it. The discussions are confined to occasional brief notes.

Most of the book is organized around Latin and Greek prefixes, roots, and suffixes, although no knowledge of Latin or Greek is necessary for mastering them. These elements are the basis of many English words, and in learning them a student will take the longest deliberate step possible in a short space of time toward an effective vocabulary. Such study often leads to an interest in other kinds of derivations, and a sampling of these is offered in the supplementary exercises, which call for dictionary work.

The book readily lends itself to study and discussion in the classroom, but it has been especially fashioned for independent use. The answer to each frame is provided on the following page (eliminating the need to cover the answers), and review exercises, also with answers, are spaced at regular intervals. Any student who wishes to strengthen his vocabulary can perform every exercise with no help other than that of a good dictionary.

Morton J. Cronin

Contents

PREFACE   v

INTRODUCTION: TO THE STUDENT   ix

1. LATIN PREFIXES   1
2. ASSIMILATION OF LATIN PREFIXES   39
3. LATIN SUFFIXES   101
4. LATIN NUMBERS   131
5. LATIN ROOTS   79
6. GREEK PREFIXES   58
7. GREEK SUFFIXES   74
8. GREEK NUMBERS   96
9. GREEK ROOTS   44

LATIN PREFIXES: Review 1   137
LATIN PREFIXES: Review 2   139
LATIN PREFIXES: Review 3   141
LATIN NUMBERS: Review   143

LATIN ROOTS: Review 1	**145**
LATIN ROOTS: Review 2	**147**
LATIN ROOTS: Review 3	**149**
LATIN ROOTS: Review 4	**151**
LATIN ROOTS: Review 5	**153**
LATIN ROOTS: Review 6	**155**
GREEK PREFIXES: Review	**157**
GREEK NUMBERS: Review	**159**
GREEK ROOTS: Review 1	**161**
GREEK ROOTS: Review 2	**163**
GREEK ROOTS: Review 3	**165**
WORDS FROM THE NAMES OF PEOPLE	**167**
WORDS FROM THE NAMES OF PLACES	**169**
WORDS FROM THE NAMES OF CHARACTERS IN FICTION	**171**
WORDS FROM THE NAMES OF MYTHOLOGICAL CHARACTERS	**173**

Introduction: To the Student

Everyone has in his vocabulary words that he recognizes when he sees them in print but that he would have a hard time defining accurately and would feel insecure in using in his own writing or speech. We may know, for example, that the words *euphony* and *resonant* both have something to do with sound, more specifically something favorable, without being able to use them with confidence.

One reason for this uncertainty is that we have not grown up with these words. They are not part of the everyday vocabulary we learn as children, a vocabulary that stems largely from Old English, the Germanic tongue of those tribes, chiefly Angles and Saxons, that invaded England in the fifth century and drove out the native population.

Rather, they are part of that vocabulary that we acquire only in later life and with conscious effort. And it so happens that this second vocabulary consists mostly of words derived from Latin (either directly or through the Romance languages, especially French) and from Greek (either directly or through Latin). Thousands of such words entered English with the Christianization of England, the Norman Conquest, the Renaissance, and the continued influence, still operating to this day, of the Greek and Roman civilizations in general. By the time these words get into our heads, however, the simple words of childhood are in our bones. If, like the Germans, we had developed fully the habit of creating new words by combining familiar ones, the ideas expressed in words like *euphony, resonant, cosmopolite,* and *valedictory* would have materialized in some such terms as *goodsound, soundingagainandagain, worldcitizen,* and *goodbyespeech.* Nobody would have any trouble with these words. Essentially, all one does when he has a knowledge of Latin and Greek word elements is to translate them into simple English, at least until the new words from Latin and Greek become thoroughly familiar.

In this country a person's grammar and pronunciation do not reveal the extent of his education as obviously as they do in many other countries. In America it is primarily differences in vocabulary which reveal differences in education. This does not mean that educated Americans confine themselves to words of Latin and Greek origin—far from it. It does mean, however, that their knowledge of such words is extensive and that they use them when they need them.

Every level of English has its legitimate and effective uses. The person who speaks or writes well is the person who can command the resources of English at all its levels and can thus fit the right word to a particular situation. *Swinish* is the right word under certain circumstances, but *porcine* might be more apt under other circumstances. Everybody knows how to use the word *wrongdoer,* but at times the more desirable term is *transgressor.* We shall concentrate on reviewing the elite verbal troops of Rome and Greece, but only because they are the ones we need practice in commanding, not because we wish to diminish respect for the familiar soldiers of common usage—tough and durable, often piquant and expressive—without which English would not be the wonderfully versatile language it is.

Our study will be principally concerned with Latin and Greek prefixes, roots, and suffixes. A *root* is that part of a word which expresses its basic meaning, as distinguished from the formative parts which modify this meaning. The formative parts may precede the root, in which case they are called *prefixes,* or they may come after it, in which case they are called *suffixes.* In the word *reformation,* for instance, *form* is the root; *re-*, meaning "again," is the prefix; and *-ation* is the suffix by means of which the word is made a noun.

Learning the prefixes in the exercises that follow is a preparation for the exercises on roots, which will involve study of both prefixes and roots. But learning prefixes is also an end in itself. If you know what the prefix of an unfamiliar word means, you can often guess the meaning of the word, especially if you find it in context, even if you do not know the meaning of its root. If you know, for instance, that one of the meanings of *ex-* is "out," you will not have much difficulty in grasping the meaning in context of *excavate, excision, excrete, exhume, expropriate, expunge, extirpate, extradite, extrude,* and *exude.*

The words which the exercises on roots call for will often contain prefixes as well as roots, and occasionally more than one of either. For instance, if there were exercises for the Latin root *pos*, which means "put" or "place," they might call for such words as *pose* (one root), *depose* (one prefix and one root), *decompose* (two prefixes and one root), and *juxtapose* (two roots).

As for suffixes, their function is explained in the body of the text. Only a few exercises will be devoted to them, for they seldom pose a problem for anyone whose native language is English.

You will have at least some familiarity with many of the words taken up in this book, and you are expected to guess as many answers as you can. One of your purposes in using this book is to learn new words, but your main purpose is to learn the meanings of the prefixes, roots, and suffixes—or to become more fully conscious of their meanings—in order to use familiar words with greater confidence and grasp unfamiliar words that contain these elements.

If you cannot guess or infer the correct answer for a question, you will find it by turning the page. If you need practice in looking up words, however, try to find in the dictionary the word or definition called for before reading the answer in the book.

Most of this book is made up of *frames,* in each of which you will be asked to do one of two things:

1. Complete an unfinished sentence by writing the word that the sentence defines or suggests.

Example: When an individual is compelled to give up a throne or other high position, we say that he has been deposed   .

2. Write an answer to a question about a particular word.

Example: When two items have been *juxtaposed* to one another, what has been done with them?
 They have been placed side by side.

(In the second type of frame it is not expected that your answer will match word for word the answer in the book.)

The exercises begin with Frame 1 on page 3. When you have finished Frame 1, move to Frame 2, which is in the same position on the next right-hand page (page 5). You will find the right answer to Frame 1 in the box to the left of Frame 2. If your answer is not correct, or if you were not able to furnish an answer, turn back to Frame 1 and correct it or write in what is missing. The answer for a frame will always be presented in the box to the left of the following frame.

Continue through the book until you reach the end, taking *only* the top gray frame on each right-hand page (7, 9, 11, 13, etc.). When you reach the end of the book, return to page 1 and follow the second band—this one is white—through the book, still working only on the right-hand pages. Continue in this way through the third, fourth, fifth, sixth, and seventh bands.

When you reach the last band on the last right-hand page (Frame 450), return to page 2 and begin reading the gray bands at the top of the left-hand pages. The last frame is 835 on page 134. Altogether, you will have gone through the book fourteen times.

At regular intervals throughout the book you will be directed to one of the Review Exercises. These will give you a chance to check on your progress. The answers are on the back of each Review Exercise page.

At the end of the book are sets of exercises on Words from Names of People, Words from Names of Places, Words from Names of Characters in Fiction, and Words from Names of Mythological Characters. These exercises are not programed, nor are the answers provided. You are to use the dictionary to find both the words and their meanings from the information given. The purpose of these exercises is not only to add more words to your vocabulary but to point up a few more of the many sources of the English vocabulary.

VOCABULARY 1000

1 Latin Prefixes

(Frames 1–147)

INTRA–, INTRO–, *into, within*
Commerce between states is interstate commerce. Commerce within the boundaries of one state is <u>INTRASTATE</u> commerce.

65

---

semiskilled

SEMI–, *half, partly*
The series of contests that immediately precedes the final series in an athletic tournament is called the <u>SEMIFINALS</u>.

128 / 129

---

uniform

UNI, *one*
Whatever is the only one of its kind is <u>UNIQUE</u>.

183 / 184

Those that live in water.

AQUA, AQUE, *water*
Why are certain solutions called *aqueous* solutions?

<u>THEY ARE WATERY SOLUTIONS</u>

249 / 250

---

malefactor

FAC, FACT, *make, do*
The root *ol* means "smell." An individual's sense of smell depends on his <u>OLFACTORY</u> organs.

316 / 317

---

delineate

LINE, *line*
Using the prefix INTER–, finish this sentence: Notes inserted between the lines of a text are <u>INTERLINEAR</u> notes.

383 / 384

page 1

An agreement reached by three parties. 450	**PASS**, *feel* An individual who feels intensely or ardently is a _PASSIONATE_ individual. 451
The two groups become similar. 516	**SIMIL, SIMUL**, *like, similar* The root *ver* means "true." When a critic says of a story, play, or novel that it possesses *verisimilitude*, what does he mean? _SEEMS TRUE TO LIFE._ 517
invertebrates 581	**VERT, VERS**, *turn* If a person constantly *adverts* to a subject, what does he do? _CONSTANTLY REFERS TO THE SUBJECT._ 582
A voice that sounds pleasant. 645	**EU—**, *good* The root *thanas*, a variant of *thanat*, means "death." If you believe in painlessly inducing death in the victims of painful and incurable diseases, you believe in _EUTHANASIA_. 646
tetrameter 707	**PENTA**, *five* The root *gon* means "angle" or "corner." The headquarters of the U.S. Department of Defense is located in a building called the _PENTAGON_. 708
dynasty 770	**DYNA**, *power* The root *aero* means "air." The science that studies, among other things, the forces exerted by air and the effect of these forces on airborne objects is known as _AERODYNAMICS_. 771
homonyms 835	**ONYM**, *name, meaning, pronunciation* The root *heter* means "different." Words which are different in pronunciation and meaning but the same in spelling—e.g., *lead* (verb) and *lead* (noun)—are _HETERONYMS_. 836

page 2

AB—, ABS—, *from, away*
Whatever differs from the *normal* is ___ABNORMAL___.

1

---

intrastate

INTRA—, INTRO—, *into, within*
An extrovert is an outgoing person. The opposite kind of person is an ___INTROVERT___.

65   66

---

semifinals

SEMI—, *half, partly*
Such gems as garnets, amethysts, and opals are not classified as precious stones but rather as ___SEMIPRECIOUS___ stones.

129   130

---

unique

UNI, *one*
A creature which consists of one cell—the amoeba, for example—is a ___UNICELLUAR___ creature.

184   185

Because they are watery solutions.

AQUA, AQUE, *water*
Why is a certain constellation of stars called *Aquarius*?

250   251

---

olfactory

FAC, FACT, *make, do*
The root *simil* means "like" or "similar." If you make a *facsimile* of an original work, what do you make?

317   318

---

interlinear

LINE, *line*
The root *recti* means "straight." A figure whose lines are straight is _____.

384   page 3   385

passionate	**PASS**, *feel* Using the prefix COM–, what is another word for *pity* or *sympathy*? _Compassion_
451	452
He means it seems true to life.	**SON**, *sound* A short verse form, of which Petrarch and Shakespeare are the outstanding masters, is the _Sonnet_.
517	518
He constantly refers to the subject.	**VIS, VID**, *see* Anything that can be seen is _Visible_.
582	583
euthanasia	**EU–**, *good* When a person is in a state of *euphoria*, how does he feel? _feels very good._
646	647
Pentagon	**PENTA**, *five* The root *athlon* means "a contest." In the Olympic games, the contest in which each contestant competes in five different events is called the _pentathlon_.
708	709
aerodynamics	**DYNA**, *power* The root *thermo* means "heat." The science that studies the forces exerted by heat and the conversion of these forces into mechanical energy is called _____.
771	772
heteronyms	**ONYM**, *name, meaning, pronunciation* The root *pseud* means "fictitious." A fictitious name, such as writers sometimes assume—*Mark Twain* is an example—is a _____.

abnormal 1	**AB—, ABS—,** *from, away* If you refuse to participate in an activity, such as drinking or smoking, you ___ABSTAIN___ from it. 2
introvert 66	**INTRA—, INTRO—,** *into, within* The root *ven* means "vein." An injection in a vein is an _____ injection. 67
semiprecious 130	**SEMI—,** *half, partly* How often does a *semiannual* event occur? 131
unicellular 185	**UNI,** *one* Every state in America except one has a two-house, or bicameral, legislature. Nebraska, which is the exception, has a one-house, or _____, legislature. 186
Because its outline supposedly suggests a man pouring water. 251	**ARM,** *weapon, arm* A place in which arms are stored is an _____ . 252
You make an exact copy of the original work. 318	**FAC, FACT,** *make, do* What do we mean when we refer to a person, employed by some organization, as a general *factotum*? 319
rectilinear 385	**LINE,** *line* The root *curvi* means "curved." A figure whose lines are curved is _____ . 386

page 5

compassion 452	**PASS**, *feel* Using the prefix DIS—, finish this statement: An examination of facts that is free of emotion or partiality is a _____ examination. 453
sonnet 518	**SON**, *sound* An instrumental composition in three or four movements—Mozart, Beethoven, and Brahms wrote many famous ones—is the _____. 519
visible 583	**VIS, VID**, *see* A long or comprehensive view—of a landscape, for instance—is a _____. 584
He feels very good, perhaps abnormally so. 647	**EU—**, *good* In the choice of words, some people—and all of us on occasion—prefer *euphemisms* (e.g., *inebriated*, instead of *drunk*). What is a *euphemism*? 648
pentathlon 709	**PENTA**, *five* What part of the Bible is known as the *Pentateuch*? 710
thermodynamics 772	**GAM**, *marriage* Beginning with MONO, complete this statement: If you have only one husband or wife at a time, you are a _____. 773
pseudonym 837	**ONYM**, *name, meaning, pronunciation* The root *crypt* means "secret." A secret name, such as one might assume in an illegal or clandestine organization, is a _____. 838

abstain	**AB—, ABS—**, *from, away* When a person gives up power or responsibility, such as a king who renounces his throne, he _____ABDICATES_____ it.
2	3
intravenous	**INTRA—, INTRO—**, *into, within* The root *spect* means "to look." An individual given to self-analysis is an _____ individual.
67	68
Every half year.	**SUPER—**, *above, beyond* A highway for high-speed, through traffic is usually called a freeway, an expressway, or a _____ .
131	132
unicameral	**DU**, *two* A contest between two individuals is a _____ .
186	187
armory	**ARM**, *weapon, arm* When warring parties cease hostilities and put down their arms, they proclaim an _____ .
252	253
We mean he performs many different tasks.	**FAC, FACT**, *make, do* What kind of law—unconstitutional in America—is an *ex post facto* law?
319	320
curvilinear	**LINE**, *line* What do we usually refer to when we speak of a person's *lineaments*?
386	387

page 7

dispassionate	**PASS,** *feel* What do we mean when we say that a face—that of a professional gambler, for instance—is *impassive*?
453	454
sonata	**SON,** *sound* A voice which is rich and vibrant may be called either *sonorous* or, using the prefix RE—, _____ .
519	520
vista	**VIS, VID,** *see* A device for protecting or shading the eyes—from the sun, let us say—is a _____ .
584	585
A word that says delicately what another word would say bluntly.	**EXO—, EC—, EX—** (before vowels), *out, outside* Things which are strikingly unusual, particularly if they are foreign and esthetically exciting, are _____ .
648	649
The first five books of the Old Testament.	**PENTA,** *five* If most of the lines of a poem contain five measures—the meter that occurs most often in English poetry—the poem is written in _____ .
710	711
monogamist	**GAM,** *marriage* The root *poly* means "many." If you have more than one husband or wife at a time, you are a _____ .
773	774
cryptonym	**OPT, OPS,** *eye, view* A mirage is an _____ illusion.
838	839

page 8

abdicates	**AB—, ABS—,** *from, away* The root *duct* means "to lead." When you take a person away illegally and against his will, you kidnap, or _____ABDUCT_____, him.
introspective	**INTRA—, INTRO—,** *into, within* The root *mur* means "wall." Where schools and colleges are concerned, what are *intramural* sports?
superhighway	**SUPER—,** *above, beyond* Any event which cannot be attributed to natural causes, such as a miracle, is a _____SUPERNATURAL_____ event.
duel	**DU,** *two* If an airplane has two sets of controls—an airplane for teaching beginners how to fly, for instance—we say that it has _____DUAL_____ controls.
armistice	**ARM,** *weapon, arm* The fleet of warships that Spain dispatched against England in Elizabethan times is known in history as the Spanish _____ .
A law which makes acts committed before the law was passed illegal and punishable.	**FID,** *faith* Another word for *faithfulness* is _____ .
We usually refer to the features, or lines, of his face.	**LOC,** *place* The engine that moves a train from place to place is a _____ .

page 9

We mean that it reveals no feeling.	**PASS**, *feel* What does the italicized word mean in this sentence: At the Democratic Convention in 1896, William Jennings Bryan delivered an *impassioned* speech. STRONG FEELING
resonant	**SON**, *sound* Using the prefix DIS—, what is a word that describes inharmonious sounds, such as those characteristic of much modern music? DISSONANT
visor	**VIS, VID**, *see* Using the prefix E—, complete this sentence: Whatever is easy to see or understand is ___EVIDENT___ .
exotic	**EXO—, EC—, EX—** (before vowels), *out, outside* A departure, especially by a large number of people, such as that of the Israelites from Egypt or the Mormons from Illinois, is often called an ___EXODUS___ .
pentameter	**HEXA**, *six* If a line of verse contains six measures, it is written in ___hexameter___ .
polygamist	**GAM**, *marriage* The root *miso* means "hate." An individual who hates marriage is a ___MISOGAMIST___ .
optical	**OPT, OPS**, *eye, view* A person who simply makes or sells glasses is an ___OPTICIAN___ .

abduct

AB—, ABS—, *from, away*
The root *jur* means "to swear." If you give up certain rights, practices, or opinions—especially if you do so in a formal or public statement—you _____ABJURE_____ them.

Those that involve players or teams of a single school or college.

MIS—, *wrong*
If you calculate erroneously, you _____MISCALCULATE_____.

supernatural

SUPER—, *above, beyond*
That part of a structure above its foundation—e.g., on a ship, that part which is above the main deck—is called the _____SUPERSTRUCTURE_____.

dual

DU, *two*
In music, a composition for two performers is a _____DUET_____.

Armada

ARM, *weapon, arm*
A creature protected by a covering of armorlike, jointed plates, often found in Texas and Mexico, is the _____ARMADILLO_____.

fidelity

FID, *faith*
Using the prefix IN—, think of another word for *unfaithfulness*.
_____INFIDELITY_____

locomotive

LOC, *place*
A word that designates a particular place or area is _____LOCATION_____.
(Any one of four different words beginning with LOC will complete this sentence.)

page 11

Full of strong feeling.

455

PATER, PATR, *father, fatherland*
Your ancestors on your father's side are called your _____ _____ ancestors.

456

dissonant

521

SON, *sound*
What do we mean when we say that several voices cried out in *unison*?

522

evident

586

VIS, VID, *see*
Using the prefix SUPER—, finish this sentence: If you oversee or direct the work of others, you _____ it.

587

exodus

650

EXO—, EC—, EX— (before vowels), *out, outside*
A person who is beside himself with happiness is an _____ person.

651

hexameter

712

HEXA, *six*
The root *pod* means "foot." An animal with six feet—any insect, for instance—is a _____ .

713

misogamist

775

GAM, *marriage*
Using the prefix EXO—, finish this statement: Sociologists refer to the practice of marrying outside one's own tribal, social, or religious group as _____ .

776

optician

840

OPT, OPS, *eye, view*
A person who examines eyes, measures vision, and fits glasses is an _____ .

page 12

841

abjure	**AB—, ABS—,** *from, away* The root *rad* means "to scrape." When something has been *abraded*—the image on an old coin, for instance—what has happened to it? *SCRAPED OR WORN AWAY*
5	6
miscalculate	**MIS—,** *wrong* If you put the wrong construction on a statement or remark, you _____ it.
70	71
superstructure	**SUPER—,** *above, beyond* Whatever is matchless in quality is _____ .
134	135
duet	**DU,** *two* A house with separate living quarters for two families is commonly called a _____ .
189	190
armadillo	**ARM,** *weapon, arm* A metal framework of supporting arms used in modeling clay is an _____ .
255	256
infidelity	**FID,** *faith* Again using the prefix IN—, finish this statement: An individual who does not believe in a certain religion is sometimes referred to by those who do believe in it as an _____ .
322	323
location *or* locality *or* locale *or* locus	**LOC,** *place* If a disturbance is confined to a relatively small area, it is _____ .
389	390

paternal

PATER, PATR, *father, fatherland*
Another word for *fatherhood* is _____ .

We mean they cried out together (i.e., as if they were one voice).

SON, *sound*
If *supersonic* speed is speed greater than that of sound, what is *subsonic* speed?

---

supervise

VIS, VID, *see*
Using the prefix EN—, finish this statement: If you form a picture of something in your mind, you _____ it.
(Either of two different words containing VIS will complete this sentence.)

---

ecstatic

EXO—, EC—, EX— (before vowels), *out, outside*
The root *zema* means "to boil." A disease in which inflamed sores ooze, or boil, out of the skin is called _____ .

---

hexapod

HEPTA, *seven*
The root *archy* means "government." The seven kingdoms into which England was divided after the Anglo-Saxon invasion—Essex, Kent, Mercia, etc.—are known in history as the _____ .

---

exogamy

GAM, *marriage*
The root *endo* means "within." Sociologists refer to the practice of marrying within one's own group as _____ .

---

optometrist

OPT, OPS, *eye, view*
Using the prefix SYN—, complete this statement: If you condense or summarize a lengthy document so that you can view its main features together, you produce a _____ .

page 14

It has been scraped, or worn, away.	**AB—, ABS—,** *from, away* When a country decides to *abrogate* a treaty, what does it decide to do? ANNUL OR CANCEL THE TREATY
misconstrue	**MIS—,** *wrong* When you fail to apprehend the real significance of something, you are the victim of a _____.
superlative	**SUPER—,** *above, beyond* A person in charge of the activity of others is commonly called a _____. (Either of two different words beginning with SUPER— will complete this sentence.)
duplex	**DU,** *two* Another word for deception or double-dealing is _____.
armature	**CARN,** *flesh* A popular pink flower that takes its name from this root is the _____.
infidel	**FID,** *faith* Using the prefix CON—, complete this sentence: Information which you impart only to someone in whose discretion you have faith is _____ information.
localized	**LOC,** *place* Using the prefix RE—, finish this statement: After a time of troubles in Illinois, many Mormons _____ in what is now Utah.

page 15

paternity 457	**PATER, PATR,** *father, fatherhood* An individual, usually a wealthy one, who sponsors and supports some person or organization is often called a _____ . 458
A speed less than that of sound. 523	**SPEC, SPECT,** *look* An individual who observes an event without participating in it is a _____ . 524
envision *or* envisage 588	**VIS, VID,** *see* When a person experiences a *prevision*, what happens? 589
eczema 652	**EXO—, EC—, EX—** (before vowels), *out, outside* The root *tomy* means "to cut." What, then, is an *appendectomy*? 653
Heptarchy 714	**HEPTA,** *seven* What part of the Bible is called the *Heptateuch*? 715
endogamy 777	**GEO,** *earth* Information concerning the location of cities, countries, mountains, rivers, etc. is _____ information. 778
synopsis 842	**OPT, OPS,** *eye, view* Again using the prefix SYN—, finish this sentence: Three of the four Gospels of the New Testament, those of Matthew, Mark, and Luke, present much the same view of Christ. Consequently, they are called the _____ Gospels. 843

page 16

It decides to annul, or cancel, the treaty. 7	**ANTE—**, *before* A waiting *room* is also called an ___ANTEROOM___ . 8
misapprehension 72	**MIS—**, *wrong* An improper alliance, especially a marriage between two people who are not suited to one another, is called a _____ . 73
supervisor *or* superintendent 136	**SUPER—**, *above, beyond* The root *script* means "to write." In a letter, what does the *superscription* usually consist of? 137
duplicity 191	**TRI**, *three* A figure with three sides and three angles is a _____ . 192
carnation 257	**CARN**, *flesh* A highly seasoned dish of Mexican origin which consists, among other things, of chili with meat is known as chili con _____ . 258
confidential 324	**FID**, *faith* Again using the prefix CON—, finish this sentence: A close friend in whom you confide is your _____ . 325
relocated 391	**LOC**, *place* Using the prefix AL—, finish this sentence: The government _____ funds for the relief of tornado victims. 392

page 17

patron 458	**PATER, PATR,** *father, fatherland* An estate inherited from one's father or another ancestor is a _____ . 459
spectator 524	**SPEC, SPECT,** *look* A remarkable sight which attracts onlookers is a _____ . 525
He foresees some future event. 589	**VIS, VID,** *see* Why do we refer to a person—one who spends too much money, for example—as *improvident*? 590
A cutting out of the appendix. 653	**EXO—, EC—, EX—** (before vowels), *out, outside* When the moon comes between the sun and the earth, thus blotting out the sun, this event is known as a solar _____ . 654
The first seven books of the Old Testament. 715	**OCT,** *eight* The marine animal with eight arms is called an _____ . 716
geographical 778	**GEO,** *earth* Information concerning the nature and history of the earth's structure is _____ information. 779
Synoptic 843	**OPT, OPS,** *eye, view* The root *thanat* means "death." William Cullen Bryant wrote a famous poem in which he presented his view of death. He entitled the poem _____ . 844

page 18

anteroom 8	**ANTE—**, *before* When the *date* of one event comes before that of another, the first event ___ANTE DATES___ the second. 9
misalliance 73	**MIS—**, *wrong* The root *nom* means "name." The wrong name for anything is a _____ . 74
The address and the date (written above the main body of the letter). 137	**SUPER—**, *above, beyond* What kind of person merits the term *supercilious*? 138
triangle 192	**TRI**, *three* A set of three, especially three musicians who perform together, is called a _____ . 193
carne 258	**CARN**, *flesh* The season of festivities before Lent, when Christians in one last revelry say farewell to the flesh, is called the _____ season. 259
confidant 325	**FID**, *faith* Using the prefix AF—, complete this statement: In law, a written statement made under oath, often before a notary public, is called an _____ . 326
allocated 392	**LOC**, *place* Why are such words as *reckon, patio,* and *coulee* called *localisms*? 393

page 19

patrimony 459	**PATER, PATR**, *father, fatherland* Using the prefix EX—, complete this sentence: An individual who has left his native land, whether his departure was forced or voluntary, is an _____ . 460
spectacle 525	**SPEC, SPECT**, *look* An item inspected as an example of its class or type is a _____ . 526
Because he does not see or plan ahead. 590	**VIT**, *life* Among the pills people take to increase their vigor, the most popular nowadays are _____ pills. 591
eclipse 654	**EXO—, EC—, EX—** (before vowels), *out, outside* The root *centr* means "center." An individual whose behavior is out of the ordinary is an _____ individual. 655
octopus 716	**OCT**, *eight* A figure with eight angles is an _____ . 717
geological 779	**GEO**, *earth* The name of that branch of mathematics first systematized by Euclid is _____ . 780
Thanatopsis 844	Before proceeding to Frame 845, do Review 2 on page 163.

antedates	**ANTE—**, *before* A.M. is an abbreviation for ___ANTI MERIDIEM___.
misnomer	**MIS—**, *wrong* When a person is convicted of a *misdemeanor*, what is he convicted of?
An arrogant or haughty person.	**TRANS—**, *across, through, beyond* A liner that crosses the *Atlantic* is a _____ liner.
trio	**TRI**, *three* The French flag, which possesses three broad areas of color, is commonly known as the _____ .
carnival	**CARN**, *flesh* Animals that eat plants are called *herbivorous*. Those that eat flesh are called _____ .
affidavit	**FID**, *faith* The Latin word *bona* means "good." An offer made in good faith—an offer of marriage, say—is a bona _____ offer.
Because their use is mostly confined to certain areas or regions.	**LOQ, LOCUT**, *speak* A person who likes to talk, especially one who talks excessiv[ely] _____ .

page 21

expatriate

460

PATER, PATR, *father, fatherland*
Using the prefix RE—, complete this statement: People who have been returned to their native land—for example, after the conclusion of a war—have been _____ .

461

specimen

526

SPEC, SPECT, *look*
Using the prefix PER—, finish this statement: A man who judges a situation without seeing or sufficiently appreciating all the important elements in it lacks _____ .

527

vitamin

591

VIT, *life*
A person who tires easily is one who lacks _____ .

592

eccentric

655

EXO—, EC—, EX— (before vowels), *out, outside*
What happens to evil spirits when they are *exorcised*?

656

octagon

717

ENNEA, *nine*
This item is included only for the sake of completeness. The English words in which it appears—*ennead, enneagon, enneasyllabic,* etc.—rarely occur.

718

GEO, *earth*
A first name for a man which means "tiller of the earth" is
_____ .

781

PAN, *all*
The international agency created to encourage cooperation among all the North and South *American* republics is called the _____
_____ Union.

page 22

845

ante meridiem	**ANTE—**, *before* The root *ced* means "to go." When someone, in discussing your family, speaks of your *antecedents*, what is he speaking of? *YOUR ANCESTORS*
A breach of the law (but a minor one, as compared with a felony or capital crime).	**MIS—**, *wrong* When are you justified in calling an individual a *miscreant*?
transatlantic	**TRANS—**, *across, through, beyond* A train that crosses a *continent* is a _____ train.
tricolor	**TRI**, *three* The root *sect* means "to cut." If you cut or divide something into three parts, you _____ it.
carnivorous	**CARN**, *flesh* Using the prefix IN—, finish this sentence: When an individual embodies some characteristic to an extraordinary degree—prudence or courage, for example—we often say he is the very _____ of that characteristic.
fide	**FID**, *faith* A variant form of DIS— is DIF—. What sort of person is a *diffident* person?
loquacious	**LOQ, LOCUT**, *speak* Using the prefix E—, complete this sentence: An individual who speaks fluently and effectively is _____.

page 23

repatriated	**PATER, PATR**, *father, fatherland* What kind of society is a *patriarchal* society?
461	462
perspective	**SPEC, SPECT**, *look* Using the prefix PRO—, finish this sentence: The descriptive statement that a new company issues, chiefly for the benefit of potential investors, is called a _____.
527	528
vitality	**VIT**, *life* Important statistics concerning people, especially large population groups, are called _____ statistics.
592	593
They are driven out.	**EXO—, EC—, EX—** (before vowels), *out, outside* If you subject a literary work to *exegesis*—this word is used especially in connection with Biblical studies—what do you subject it to?
656	657
	DEC, *ten* A period of ten years is a _____.
	719
George	**GEO**, *earth* Six kings of England have possessed this name. In the eighteenth century, during the reigns of the first two, a style of architecture first developed called _____.
781	782
Pan American	**PAN**, *all* A movement whose purpose is to unite all *Slavic* peoples is a _____ movement.
845	846

page 24

Your ancestors.

11

ANTE—, *before*
The root *bell* means "war." What is a person talking about when he refers to the *antebellum* South?

SOUTH BEFORE THE CIVIL WAR

12

When he is an evil person.

76

NON—, *not, without*
One who does not conform with his society is a _____ .

77

---

transcontinental

140

TRANS—, *across, through, beyond*
If you can see through something, it is _____ .

141

---

trisect

195

TRI, *three*
The root *dent* means "tooth." The instrument with three teeth or prongs associated with Neptune is called a _____ .

196

---

incarnation

261

CARN, *flesh*
Using the prefixes RE— and IN—, complete this statement: If you believe that after death the soul returns and inhabits another body, you believe in _____ .

262

One who is shy, apparently without much faith in himself.

328

FID, *faith*
What is a *fiduciary* institution?

329

---

eloquent

395

LOQ, LOCUT, *speak*
Again using the prefix E—, complete this statement: The art of public speaking is often referred to as the art of _____ .

page 25

396

A society ruled by fathers (or men). 462	**PATER, PATR,** *father, fatherland* When an individual visits another country and associates with his *compatriots,* who does he associate with? 463
prospectus 528	**SPEC, SPECT,** *look* What is wrong with a *specious* line of reasoning? *plausible* 529
vital 593	**VIT,** *life* Using the prefix RE—, complete this sentence: When, after a period of fatigue, you feel a return of vigor, you feel _____. 594
You subject it to interpretation— i.e., you bring the meaning out. 657	**HYPER—,** *excessive* An individual who is excessively *sensitive* is _____. 658
decade 719	**DEC,** *ten* The root *athlon* means "a contest." In the Olympic games, the contest in which each contestant competes in ten different events is called the _____. 720
Georgian 782	**GEO,** *earth* Virgil, the most famous Roman poet, wrote a series of poems on agricultural life called the _____. 783
Pan-Slavic 846	**PAN,** *all* A word, first coined by Milton in *Paradise Lost,* that means a scene of wild and clamorous disorder, such as the rioting of every *demon* in hell might create, is _____. 847

page 26

The South before the Civil War. 12	**BI—**, *two, twice* A pair of glasses whose lenses have been ground for both close vision and distant vision are called ___bifocals___. 13
nonconformist 77	**NON—**, *not, without* An officer who is not commissioned, such as a sergeant or a corporal, is a ___non commisioned___ officer. 78
transparent 141	**TRANS—**, *across, through, beyond* The root *fus* means "to pour." The removal of blood from one person to another is known as a blood _____. 142
trident 196	**QUADR**, *four* A figure or an area with four angles is a _____. 197
reincarnation 262	**CARN**, *flesh* When are we justified in asserting that someone is full of carnal impulses? 263
One that holds money or property in trust for others, such as a bank. 329	**FIGUR**, *form, shape* If a fabric is ornamented with forms and shapes, it is _____. 330
elocution 396	**LOQ, LOCUT**, *speak* Using the prefix COL—, complete this sentence: The language that is characteristic of informal—but not necessarily uneducated—conversation is called _____ language. 397

page 27

With others from his own country.

463

PEND, *hang*
When a case has not yet been decided, we usually say that it is still _____.

464

It *seems* correct, but it is not.

529

SPEC, SPECT, *look*
When you contemplate an event in *retrospect,* when do you contemplate it?

530

revitalized

594

VIT, *life*
Using the prefix DE—, finish this statement: When someone loses his strength, we commonly say that he has become _____.

595

hypersensitive

658

HYPER—, *excessive*
A person who is too *critical* is _____.

659

decathlon

720

DEC, *ten*
The root *log(ue)* means "to speak." The Ten Commandments are also known as the _____.

721

Georgics

783

GEO, *earth*
A bureau of the U.S. government maps the topographical changes that occur in America. This bureau is known as the Coast and _____ Survey.

784

pandemonium

847

PAN, *all*
Whatever purports to be a remedy for all personal or political ills is often called a _____.

848

page 28

bifocals	**BI—**, *two, twice* The root *gam* means "marriage." In this country, a man who is married to two women at the same time has committed ___bigamy___.
noncommissioned	**NON—**, *not, without* Remarks that do not commit you to anything or reveal your thoughts are _____ remarks.
transfusion	**TRANS—**, *across, through, beyond* The root *gress* means "to step." What do we mean when we say that a person has committed a *transgression*?
quadrangle	**QUADR**, *four* Four children born of the same mother at the same time are called _____.
When he is full of sensual, or fleshly, impulses.	**CARN**, *flesh* What do we mean when we speak of the *carnage* on a battlefield?
figured	**FIGUR**, *form, shape* A small carved or molded object is a _____.
colloquial	**LOQ, LOCUT**, *speak* The root *soli* means "alone." A dramatic monologue in which a character speaks to himself—several famous ones occur in *Hamlet*—is known as a _____.

page 29

pending

464

PEND, *hang*
The device that hangs from certain clocks and swings to and fro is a _____.

465

After it has occurred.

530

TEMP, TEMPOR, *time*
The speed at which a musical composition is played is called the _____.

531

---

devitalized

595

VIV, *life*
A person who is full of life is a _____ person.
(Either of two words beginning with VIV will complete this sentence.)

596

---

hypercritical

659

HYPER—, *excessive*
When an individual experiences great *tension*—e.g., when his blood pressure is too high—we say he is in a state of _____.

660

Decalogue *or* Decalog

721

HECTO, *hundred*
In the metric system, a hundred liters is a _____.

722

Geodetic

784

Before proceeding to Frame 785, do Review 1 on page 161.

---

panacea

848

PAN, *all*
The root *oram* means "a view." An all-encompassing view—one from a mountaintop, for example—is a _____ view.

849

page 30

bigamy 14	**BI—**, *two, twice* The root *sect* means "to cut." In geometry, if you divide a line into two equal parts, you ___bisect___ it. 15
noncommittal 79	**NON—**, *not, without* The root *chal* means "to care." When an individual exhibits casual indifference—for example, in the face of danger—he is _____. 80
He has gone beyond the limits of accepted behavior. 143	**TRANS—**, *across, through, beyond* When is it appropriate to refer to something—a thought or feeling, for instance—as *transitory*? 144
quadruplets 198	**QUADR**, *four* An animal with two feet is a *biped*. The word for an animal with four feet is _____. 199
We mean the dead and mutilated bodies. 264	**CORP**, *body* That body of troops in an army which usually consists of two or more divisions is known as a _____. 265
figurine 331	**FIGUR**, *form, shape* Language that consists of certain rhetorical devices which usually evoke vivid images—e.g., similes and metaphors—is called _____ language. 332
soliloquy 398	**LOQ, LOCUT**, *speak* When two or more people have a *colloquy,* what do they have? *page 31* 399

pendulum 465	**PEND,** *hang* Certain items of jewelry that hang down are called _____. 466
tempo 531	**TEMP, TEMPOR,** *time* Anything that lasts for only a short time is _____. 532
vivacious (*or* vivid) 596	**VIV,** *life* The word for operating on a living animal for experimental purposes is _____. 597
hypertension 660	**HYPER—,** *excessive* A person whose *thyroid* gland secretes excessively is suffering from a _____ condition. 661
hectoliter 722	**HECTO,** *hundred* In the same system, a hundred grams is a _____. 723
	GRAPH, GRAM, *writing, description* A soft, black carbon used in lead pencils, which received its name from the fact that one can write with it, is called _____. 785
panoramic 849	**PAN,** *all* The root *the* means "god." The doctrine which holds that God is not a personality and which simply equates Him with everything in the universe is known as _____. 850

page 32

bisect	**BI–**, *two, twice* The root *ped* means "foot." What is the word for any animal with two feet? _____biped_____
nonchalant	**NON–**, *not, without* When you call a person a *nonentity,* what do you think of him?
When it is temporary or passing.	**ULTRA–**, *exceedingly, beyond* Whatever is exceedingly *modern* is _____.
quadruped	**QUADR**, *four* An individual who speaks two languages is *bilingual.* One who speaks four languages is _____.
corps	**CORP**, *body* Another word for *fat* or *fleshy* is _____.
figurative	**FIGUR**, *form, shape* Using the prefix DIS–, what is another word for *deform*? _____
They have a conversation or conference.	**LOQ, LOCUT**, *speak* What do we mean when we say of a talkative or evasive person that his speech is full of *circumlocutions*?

page 33

pendants 466	**PEND,** *hang* Using the prefix AP—, complete this statement: Supplementary material attached to the end of a book is known as an _____.	467
temporary 532	**TEMP, TEMPOR,** *time* Using the prefix CON—, complete this statement: People who live when you do, especially those about your own age, are your _____.	533
vivisection 597	**VIV,** *life* Using the prefix RE—, complete this statement: If you put new life into something, you _____ it.	598
hyperthyroid 661	**HYPER—,** *excessive* Why is a certain rhetorical device, not intended to be taken as the literal truth, called *hyperbole*? (The statement "All men are monsters" is an example of it.)	662
hectogram 723	**KILO,** *thousand* In the metric system, a thousand meters is a _____.	724
graphite 785	**GRAPH, GRAM,** *writing, description* The arts of delineation, such as drawing, painting, engraving, and etching, are known as the _____ arts.	786
pantheism 850	**PAN,** *all* When an individual appears—on some special occasion, say—in full *panoply,* what does he appear in?	851

biped	**BI—**, *two, twice* A tooth with one point is called a *cuspid*. What is a tooth with two points called? _bicuspid_
16	17
You think he is of little or no importance.	**PER—**, *through* or *throughout, by* If something is pierced through with one or more holes, such as a sheet of stamps, it is _____ .
81	82
ultramodern	**ULTRA—**, *exceedingly, beyond* A country that is extremely *nationalistic* is _____ .
145	146
quadrilingual	**QUINT**, *five* When five children are born to the same woman at one time, they are called _____ .
200	201
corpulent	**CORP**, *body* A tiny body, such as one of the red or white cells that float in man's blood, is called a _____ .
266	267
disfigure	**FIGUR**, *form, shape* Using the prefix CON—, finish this sentence: The overall shape of an object is called its _____ .
333	334
We mean he talks around a subject, instead of coming directly to the point.	**MAGN**, *great, large* If you enlarge something, as a microscope does, you _____ it.
400	page 35 401

appendix 467	**PEND**, *hang* Again using the prefix AP—, complete this sentence: Anything attached to or hanging from the body of something is an _____ . 468
contemporaries 533	**TEMP, TEMPOR**, *time* Using the prefix EX—, complete this sentence: If you simply speak out as the particular time or occasion moves you, without special preparation, you speak _____ . 534
revive *or* revivify 598	**VIV**, *life* Using the prefix CON—, finish this sentence: A man who enjoys eating, drinking, and having a lively time with others is a _____ man. 599
Because it is an exaggerated statement made deliberately for effect. 662	**HYPO—**, *under, deficient* An individual who is less *active* than is normal is _____ . 663
kilometer 724	**KILO**, *thousand* In the same system, electrical power equal to one thousand watts is a _____ . 725
graphic 786	**GRAPH, GRAM**, *writing, description* Since these arts are associated with the vivid representation of objects, we call a verbal description that evokes a clear mental picture a _____ description. 787
He appears in all appropriate array. 851	**PATH**, *feeling, disease* An individual who arouses pity in us is a _____ individual. 852

bicuspid

17

NOTE: In such words as *biweekly* and *bimonthly,* this prefix may mean "every two"—i.e., every two weeks or every two months—or it may mean "twice"—i.e., twice a week or twice a month. Where one's own practice is concerned, the best way out of this difficulty is simply not to use those words in which the meaning of this prefix is not clear.

---

perforated

82

PER—, *through* or *throughout, by*
A businessman who receives a fixed daily allowance for expenses receives a _____ _____ allowance.

83

---

ultranationalistic

146

ULTRA—, *exceedingly, beyond*
The invisible rays beyond the *violet* end of the spectrum are the _____ rays.

147

---

quintuplets

201

QUINT, *five*
A group of five persons or things is a _____ .

202

---

corpuscle

267

CORP, *body*
Punishment inflicted on the body is _____ punishment.

268

---

configuration

334

FIGUR, *form, shape*
Using the prefix TRANS—, complete this sentence: The change in the appearance of Jesus on the mountain, as recorded by Matthew and Luke, is known as the _____ .

335

---

magnify

401

MAGN, *great, large*
Another word for *splendor* or *grandeur* is _____ .

402

appendage 468	**PEND,** *hang* Using the prefix IM—, finish this sentence: Events that are about to occur—they are hanging just over our heads, as it were—are _____ events. 469
extempore *or* extemporaneously 534	**TEMP, TEMPOR,** *time* What does the italicized expression mean in the following sentence: The Vice President acts as the President of the U.S. Senate, but in his absence a Senator is made President *pro tempore*. 535
convivial 599	**VOC, VOK,** *call* A man's profession or calling is his _____. 600
hypoactive 663	**HYPO—,** *under, deficient* A person whose *thyroid* gland secretes deficiently is suffering from a _____ condition. 664
kilowatt 725	NOTE: In the metric system, the Greek *deca* or *deka* means ten, as in decameter (10 meters), and the Latin *deci* means one tenth, as in decimeter (1/10 of a meter). The Greek root *hecto* is used to designate one hundred, as in hectometer (100 meters), while the Latin *centi* is used to mean one hundredth, as in centimeter (1/100 of a meter).
graphic 787	**GRAPH, GRAM,** *writing, description* A message sent by cable is a _____. 788
pathetic 852	**PATH,** *feeling, disease* If a situation or an artistic work evokes much sadness or compassion in us, we commonly say that it is full of _____. 853

page 38

	CIRCUM–, *around* The line around a circle is its <u>circumference</u>.
	18
per diem *or* per day 83	**PER–**, *through* or *throughout*, *by* A plant that lives year after year is called a _____ plant. 84
ultraviolet 147	# 2 Assimilation of Latin Prefixes (Frames 148–169)
quintet 202	**SEX**, *six* A group of six is a _____ . 203
corporal 268	**CORP**, *body* Legal terminology includes many words taken from Latin. The expression that means "body of the crime" is _____ delicti. 269
Transfiguration 335	**FLEX, FLECT**, *bend, turn* If you bend your arm, you _____ it. 336
magnificence 402	**MAGN**, *great, large* In astronomy, the brightest stars are called stars of the first _____ . 403

page 39

impending

469

PEND, *hang*
What do we mean when we call something—the belly of a fat and aged man, for instance—*pendulous*?

470

For the time being.

535

TEMP, TEMPOR, *time*
When, pressed to make a decision, a person *temporizes,* what does he do?

536

vocation

600

VOC, VOK, *call*
A singer is sometimes referred to as a _____.

601

hypothyroid

664

HYPO—, *under, deficient*
Anyone who pretends to virtues he does not possess, who acts under pretense, is a _____ .

665

Another Greek root, *kilo,* means one thousand in this system, as in kilometer (1000 meters), and the Latin *milli* signifies one thousandth, as in millimeter (1/1000 of a meter).

cablegram

788

GRAPH, GRAM, *writing, description*
Using the prefix DIA—, finish this statement: A line drawing made for explanatory purposes is a _____ .

789

pathos

853

PATH, *feeling, disease*
In medicine, a doctor who specializes in studying the physical changes caused by diseases is known as a _____ .

page 40

854

circumference	**CIRCUM—**, *around* Ferdinand Magellan organized the first expedition that <u>circumnavigated</u> the earth.

perennial	**PER—**, *through* or *throughout, by* An individual who keeps going through thick and thin is a _____ individual. (Any one of three different words beginning with PER— will complete this sentence.)

The next four prefixes (AD—, COM—, IN—, and SUB—), often undergo a partial change called assimilation, in which the prefix becomes similar to the following element. One of two things occurs: (1) the last letter of the prefix changes, usually, but not always, by becoming the same as the first letter of the following element; or (2) the last letter of the prefix disappears. The word *assimilation* itself illustrates the first possibility. It springs from the prefix AD—, meaning "to" or "toward" and the root SIMIL, meaning "like" or "similar," but the last letter of the prefix has become the same as the first letter of the root.

The word *cooperate* illustrates the second possibility. It derives from the prefix COM—, meaning

sextet	**SEX**, *six* If a man is a *sexagenarian*, how many decades has he lived? _____

corpus	**CORP**, *body* An order which requires that a prisoner be brought before a court in order to determine the legality of his imprisonment is known as a writ of habeas _____.

flex	**FLEX, FLECT**, *bend, turn* Anything that is easily bent is _____.

magnitude	**MAGN**, *great, large* The charter of liberties which King John of England was compelled to grant in the thirteenth century is known as the _____ Carta.

page 41

We mean that
it hangs down.

470

PERSON, *person*
The employees of an organization are often referred to as its
_____ .

471

He stalls
(i.e., he plays
for time).

536

TEN, *hold*
A person who occupies a house or land, especially if he pays rent for it, is a _____ .

537

vocalist

601

VOC, VOK, *call*
Using the prefix RE—, what is a synonym for *cancel* or *rescind*?
_____

602

hypocrite

665

HYPO—, *under, deficient*
The root *derm* means "skin." A needle for injections under the skin is a _____ needle.

666

Before proceeding to Frame 726, do the Review on page 159.

diagram

789

GRAPH, GRAM, *writing, description*
Beginning with MONO, finish this sentence: When two or more letters, usually a person's initials, are interwoven to form a single emblem, they are called a _____ .

790

pathologist

854

PATH, *feeling, disease*
The literary device of providing inanimate nature with human feelings—e.g., "a brooding sky"— is called the _____ fallacy.

855

circumnavigated

CIRCUM—, *around*
The root *spect* means "to look." A careful person, one who looks around before he acts, is a ___circumspect___ person.

---

persistent *or*
persevering *or*
pertinacious

PER—, *through* or *throughout, by*
The root *cep* means "to grasp." An observant person, one who readily grasps the meaning of things, is a _____ person.

"together" or "with," and the root OPER, which means "work," but the last letter of the prefix has vanished.

In the case of AD—, the process of assimilation almost always consists in the prefix exchanging its *d* for the first letter of the element which follows it, as in *accessory, affiliate,* and *aggressive*. Consequently, when a word begins with *a* followed by a double consonant, as many words do, it is usually a case of the prefix AD— appearing in one of its assimilated forms.

Six—he is in his sixties.

SEPT, *seven*
In the old Roman calendar, what is now the ninth month of the year was the seventh month. That is why it is called _____ .

---

corpus

CORP, *body*
When we refer to man's *corporeal* existence, what are we referring to?

---

flexible

FLEX, FLECT, *bend, turn*
Using the prefix IN—, what is a word that describes anything that is not easily bent? _____

Magna

MAGN, *great, large*
The greatest European ruler of the Middle Ages was Charles I. He is usually called _____ .

page 43

personnel 471	**PERSON,** *person* An important or distinguished individual is a _____ . 472
tenant 537	**TEN,** *hold* A house or building divided into apartments for numerous families and typically overcrowded is usually known as a _____ . 538
revoke 602	**VOC, VOK,** *call* Using the prefix E—, what is a synonym for *summon* or *elicit*? _____ 603
hypodermic 666	**PARA—,** *alongside of, with* Two lines equidistant from one another at all points are _____ . 667

9   Greek Roots

(Frames 726–898)

monogram 790	**GRAPH, GRAM,** *writing, description* Again beginning with MONO, complete this statement: A scholarly treatise on some technical subject, often on one particular aspect of it, is commonly referred to as a _____ . 791
pathetic 855	**PATH,** *feeling, disease* Using the prefix SYM—, finish this sentence: If you feel for a person in trouble, you _____ with him. 856

page 44

circumspect

CIRCUM—, *around*
The root *scrib* means "to draw." If your activities are limited, as if a line had been drawn around them, they are ___circumscribed___.

---

perceptive

PER—, *through* or *throughout, by*
The root *vad* means "to go." If an individual's influence spreads throughout a group, his influence _____ the group.

AD—, *to, toward*
A word that modifies or applies to a noun is an _____.

September

SEPT, *seven*
A group of seven is a _____.

To his bodily existence, here on earth.

CORP, *body*
Why are angels called *incorporeal* beings?

---

inflexible

FLEX, FLECT, *bend, turn*
Using the prefix RE—, finish this statement: A thoughtful person, one who turns things over in his mind again and again, is a _____ person.

Charlemagne

MAGN, *great, large*
Why, in business or industry, are certain men referred to as *magnates*?

page 45

personage

PERSON, *person*
A man who is likable and presents an attractive appearance is
_____ .

tenement

TEN, *hold*
Using the prefix RE—, complete this sentence: If you easily recall what you have learned, you have a _____ memory.

evoke

VOC, VOK, *call*
Using the prefix IN—, finish this sentence: The prayer calling for God's blessing, offered at the beginning of certain church services, is called the _____ .

parallel

PARA—, *alongside of, with*
A plant or animal that lives with another plant or animal, and at the expense of its host, is a _____ .

ANTHROP, *man*
The science devoted primarily to the study of primitive peoples is called _____ .

monograph

NOTE: When this root assumes the form of GRAPHY, it may still be interpreted best as meaning "writing" or "description," as in *stenography* and *bibliography*, but it may also be interpreted best as meaning "art" or "science," as in *photography* and *cinematography*.

sympathize

PATH, *feeling, disease*
Using the prefix EM—, complete this sentence: The ability to enter into another person's feelings and ideas is called _____ .

page 46

circumscribed	**CIRCUM—**, *around* What do you do when you *circumvent* a difficulty—such as some rule or regulation? go around instead of attacking it.
pervades	**PER—**, *through* or *throughout*, *by* The root *spic* means "to see." What sort of person is a *perspicacious* person?
adjective	**AD—**, *to*, *toward* A word that modifies or applies to a verb is an _____.
septet	**SEPT**, *seven* If a man is a *septugenarian*, how many decades has he lived? _____
Because they have no bodies.	**CRED**, *believe*, *trust* When a shopkeeper sells merchandise on trust, we usually say that he sells on _____.
reflective	**FLEX, FLECT**, *bend*, *turn* The root *genu* means "knee." The act of bending the knee, as in church, is called _____.
Because they are men of much importance and power.	**MAGN**, *great*, *large* Why is a particular work of an artist, writer, or composer called his *magnum opus*?

page 47

personable 473	**PERSON**, *person* Using the prefix IM—, finish this sentence: If you make a judgment without being influenced by personal considerations, you make an _____ judgment. 474
retentive 539	**TEN**, *hold* What kind of person is a *tenacious* person? 540
invocation 604	**VOC, VOK**, *call* Using the prefix CON—, what is a word that designates a general assembly, especially in collegiate and ecclesiastical circles? _____ 605
parasite 668	**PARA—**, *alongside of, with* The root *phrase* means "to tell." If you restate in your own words something you have heard or read, you _____ it. 669
anthropology 726	**ANTHROP**, *man* Highly developed apes, those which most resemble man, are called the _____ apes. 727
	HYDR, *water* Another word for *fireplug* is _____. 792
empathy 857	**PATH**, *feeling, disease* Using the prefix A—, finish this statement: An individual who is listless, without feeling or concern, is an _____ individual. 858

You get around it (instead of attacking it directly).	**COUNTER—, CONTRA—,** *opposite, against* The opposite of a clockwise movement is a ___counterclockwise___ movement.
22	23
One whose judgment is keen, who sees through things.	**POST—,** *after* When you *date* a check or any other document after the actual time of writing it, you _____ it.
88	89
adverb	**AD—,** *to, toward* The root *vert* means "to turn." When you try to turn the public's attention toward something, especially something for sale, you _____ it.
149	150
Seven—he is in his seventies.	**OCT,** *eight* In the old Roman calendar, what is now the tenth month of the year was the eighth month. That is why it is called _____ .
207	208
credit	**CRED,** *believe, trust* A person to whom you owe money is your _____ .
273	274
genuflection	**FLU,** *flow* A person from whom words flow easily and smoothly is a _____ person.
340	341
Because it is his greatest work.	**MAL,** *bad* A general word for any ailment is _____ .
407	*page 49* counterclockwise 408

impersonal

474

PERSON, *person*
When we say of an individual that he is the very *personification* of courage, what do we mean?

475

One who holds on strongly to things.

540

TEN, *hold*
When we assert that an individual's position—in an argument, say—is not *tenable*, what do we mean?

541

---

convocation

605

VOC, VOK, *call*
Beginning with the root *equi,* complete this sentence: If a person's utterances can be interpreted as meaning equally one thing or another, his utterances are _____ .

606

---

paraphrase

669

PARA—, *alongside of, with*
Why is a certain kind of story called a *parable*?

670

---

anthropoid

727

ANTHROP, *man*
The root *phil* means "love." A person who loves mankind, especially one who gives away large sums of money, is a _____ .

728

---

hydrant

792

HYDR, *water*
A certain kind of airplane that can land and take off on water is called a _____ .

793

---

apathetic

858

PATH, *feeling, disease*
Using the prefix ANTI—, complete this sentence: If you dislike someone, you have an _____ to him.

859

counterclockwise

COUNTER—, CONTRA—, *opposite, against*
An attack made in response to an enemy's attack is a
counterattack .

postdate

POST—, *after*
If you decide to put off doing something until another time, you
_____ it.

advertise

AD—, *to, toward*
The root *mon* means "to warn." If you earnestly advise or warn
someone, you _____ him.

October

OCT, *eight*
A group of eight is an _____ .

creditor

CRED, *believe, trust*
The proofs—for example, certificates, diplomas, letters—that an
individual is what he purports to be are his _____ .

fluent

FLU, *flow*
A passage up which smoke or hot air can flow, as in a chimney,
is a _____ .

malady

MAL, *bad*
A disease, characterized by chills and fever, and transmitted by
certain mosquitoes, but formerly thought to be caused by bad air,
is named _____ .

We mean he is the very embodiment or perfect example of courage. 475	**PERSON,** *person* What does the expression *dramatis personae* designate? 476
We mean it is too weak to be held. 541	**TEN,** *hold* What do we mean when we say that the Korean War started during President Truman's *tenure* of office? 542
equivocal 606	**VOC, VOK,** *call* What kind of actions are *provocative* actions? 607
Because, along with the story, it carries a moral lesson. 670	**PARA—,** *alongside of, with* When we speak of a person's *paraphernalia*—that of a hunter or a scientist or a janitor, for example—what are we speaking of? 671
philanthropist 728	**ANTHROP,** *man* The root *mis* means "hate." A person who hates people is a _____. 729
hydroplane 793	**HYDR,** *water* Most plants require plenty of water, but the name of one plant in particular, which produces clusters of blue, pink, or white flowers, emphasizes this fact. The name is _____. 794
antipathy 859	**PATH,** *feeling, disease* The root *osteo* means "bone." A physician whose theory of medicine is based primarily on the idea that most ailments are the result of displaced bones is an _____. 860

page 52

counterattack	**COUNTER—, CONTRA—,** *opposite, against* The reformatory movement in the Roman Catholic Church which followed the Protestant Reformation is usually referred to in history as the <u>Counter</u> <u>Reformation</u>.	
24		25
postpone	**POST—,** *after* A note added to a completed letter is a _____.	
90		91
admonish	**AD—,** *to, toward* The Latin word *hominem* means "man." When an individual in an argument resorts to *ad hominem* remarks, what is he doing?	
151		152
octet	**OCT,** *eight* If a man is an *octogenarian,* how many decades has he lived? _____	
209		210
credentials	**CRED,** *believe, trust* A report that seems authentic and worthy of belief is a _____ report.	
275		276
flue	**FLU,** *flow* When conditions are changing, we commonly say that they are in a state of _____.	
342		343
malaria	**MAL,** *bad* In medicine, a tumor of a mild sort is called benign. But a dangerous tumor, one which may cause death, is called _____.	
409	page 53	410

The characters in a drama. 476	**PLAC,** *to please* or *appease* A peaceful and unruffled person is _____ . 477
We mean it started while President Truman held office. 542	**TEN,** *hold* When we refer to the *tenets* of an organization—of a church, for instance—what are we referring to? 543
Actions that call forth a response—thought, anger, counter-action, etc. 607	**VOC, VOK,** *call* What do we mean when we declare that a decision is *irrevocable*? 608
The things he keeps with him and uses in his work and everyday life. 671	**PERI—,** *about, around, near* If something comes about repeatedly, at either regular or irregular intervals, such as the eruption of a geyser, we say that it occurs _____ . 672
misanthrope *or* misanthropist 729	**ARCH,** *first, chief* In the Roman Catholic Church and in the Church of England, a chief bishop is an _____ . 730
hydrangea 794	**HYDR,** *water* One of the symptoms of rabies is an inability to swallow water or other liquids. That is why this disease is also known as _____ . 795
osteopath 860	**PHIL, PHILE,** *love* The society organized to sponsor a symphony orchestra is often called the _____ Society. 861

page 54

Counter Reformation	**COUNTER—, CONTRA—,** *opposite, against* Duplicates, corresponding items, or opposite numbers are also called ___Counterparts___ .	
25		26
postscript	**POST—,** *after* P.M. is usually an abbreviation for _____ _____ .	
91		92
Attacking his adversary rather than dealing with the subject.	**AD—,** *to, toward* What do we mean when we say, always in disgust, that a person has repeated something *ad nauseam*?	
152		153
Eight—he is in his eighties.	**NOV,** *nine* In the old Roman calendar, what is now the eleventh month of the year was the ninth month. That is why it is called _____ .	
210		211
credible	**CRED,** *believe, trust* Using the prefix IN—, think of another word for *unbelievable*. _____	
276		277
flux	**FLU,** *flow* When something continually moves up and down, such as the price of some commodity, we say that it _____ .	
343		344
malignant	**MAL,** *bad* A person full of ill will is a _____ person. (Any one of four different words beginning with MAL will complete this sentence.)	
410	page 55	411

placid

477

	PLAC, *to please* or *appease* If you appease an irate individual, you _____ him.
	478

We are referring to the beliefs held by the organization.

543

NOTE: Common variants of TEN are TAIN and TENT as in such words as *retain/retention, detain/detention, abstain/abstention.*

We mean the decision is final and cannot be revoked.

608

Before proceeding to Frame 609, do Review 6 on page 155.

periodically

672

PERI—, *about, around, near*
When, in making its revolutions, the moon or any other satellite is closest to the earth, it is at its _____ .

673

archbishop

730

ARCH, *first, chief*
The district governed by an archbishop is called an
_____ .

731

hydrophobia

795

HYDR, *water*
If the stopping power of an automobile is generated by the resistance offered when water or another liquid is forced through small holes, the automobile has _____ brakes.

796

Philharmonic

861

PHIL, PHILE, *love*
A man who habitually engages in brief love affairs is a
_____ .

page 56

862

counterparts	**COUNTER—, CONTRA—,** *opposite, against* The root *dict* means "to say." If you deny the truth of an assertion, you ___contradict___ the assertion.
post meridiem	**POST—,** *after* The root *hum* means "to bury." When a work is published *posthumously*, when is it published?
We mean that he has repeated it to a sickening extent.	**COM—,** *with, together* A sudden or startling event in a crowd of people will create a _____.
November	**NOV,** *nine* In the Roman Catholic Church, the practice of devotional exercises for nine days is called a _____.
incredible	**CRED,** *believe, trust* Using the prefix DIS—, finish this statement: If you have shown that a person cannot be believed or trusted, you have _____ him.
fluctuates	**FLU,** *flow* Using the prefix IN—, finish this sentence: The entry, especially a sudden one, of a sizable number of persons or things is frequently called an _____.
malign *or* malicious *or* malevolent *or* malignant	**MAL,** *bad* What do we mean when we assert that an individual, in handling some situation, was *maladroit*?

page 57

placate

478

PLAC, *to please* or *appease*
Using the prefix IM–, complete this sentence: An enemy who cannot be appeased is _____ .

479

TERR, TERRA, TER, *earth, land*
A dog, usually small, which was originally bred to dig and burrow in the earth for small game is the _____ .

544

6 Greek Prefixes

(Frames 609–680)

perigee

673

PERI–, *about, around, near*
What is the *perimeter* of an area?

674

archbishopric *or* archdiocese

731

ARCH, *first, chief*
An angel of the first rank is an _____ .

732

hydraulic

796

HYDR, *water*
Using the prefix DE–, finish this sentence: If the water has been removed from something—milk, for example—it has been _____ .

797

philanderer

862

PHIL, PHILE, *love*
A potion or magic charm for making someone fall in love is called a _____ .

863

contradict 27	**COUNTER—, CONTRA—,** *opposite, against* The root *mand* means "to command." What do you do when you *countermand* an order? cancel it. 28
After the author's death. 93	**POST—,** *after* The root *nat* means "born." What kind of care is *postnatal* care? 94
commotion 154	**COM—,** *with, together* An individual with whom you regularly associate in an intimate or friendly way is your _____. 155
novena 212	**DEC,** *ten* In the old Roman calendar, what is now the twelfth month of the year was the tenth month. That is why it is called _____. 213
discredited 278	**CRED,** *believe, trust* Using the prefix AC—, complete this sentence: When it has been certified that a school or college has met certain standards, the school or college is _____. 279
influx 345	**FLU,** *flow* Again using the prefix IN—, complete this sentence: A common infectious disease which usually affects the respiratory tract, induces fever, and so on is called _____. 346
We mean he was clumsy, not adroit. 412	**MAL,** *bad* When a doctor is convicted of *malpractice,* what is he convicted of? 413

page 59

implacable 479	**PLAC,** *to please* or *appease* Using the prefix COM—, finish this sentence: Anyone who is pleased with himself, especially if his self-satisfaction approaches smugness, is _____ . 480
terrier 544	**TERR, TERRA, TER,** *earth, land* The reddish-brown earthenware used for pottery, figurines, etc. is called _____ cotta. 545
	A—, AN— (before vowels), *not, without* A person who does not believe in any *moral* code cannot accurately be called immoral. Such an individual is an _____ person. 609
The outer edge of an area. 674	**PERI—,** *about, around, near* When, in respect to some subject, we discuss only *peripheral* matters, what do we discuss? 675
archangel 732	**ARCH,** *first, chief* A fiend of the first rank is an _____ . 733
dehydrated 797	**HYDR,** *water* The root *carbo* means "carbon." Those products, such as sugar and starch, whose chemical composition includes carbon and water are known as _____ . 798
philter *or* philtre 863	**PHIL, PHILE,** *love* The root *soph* means "wise." A lover of wisdom is a _____ . 864

page 60

You cancel it.

28

DE—, *off, down, the reverse*
If you remove frost from a surface, you _____ the surface.

29

The care a child and its mother get immediately after birth.

94

POST—, *after*
What generations does the word *posterity* designate?

95

---

companion

155

COM—, *with, together*
The root *merc* means "merchandise." People with merchandise to sell are engaged in _____ .

156

December

213

DEC, *ten*
A system of arithmetic based on the number ten is a _____ system.

214

---

accredited

279

CRED, *believe, trust*
When is it appropriate to call someone *credulous*?

280

---

influenza

346

FLU, *flow*
Using the prefix SUPER—, what is a word that describes anything unnecessary—the overflow, as it were? _____

347

He is convicted of the careless or improper practice of medicine.

413

MAL, *bad*
When a public official is convicted of *malfeasance* in office, what is he convicted of?

page 61

414

complacent	**POS, PON,** *place, put* The position you assume in standing, sitting, etc. is your _____.
terra	**TERR, TERRA, TER,** *earth, land* A word that designates a tract of ground, especially in military parlance, is _____ .
amoral	**A—, AN—** (before vowels), *not, without* Whatever is not *typical* is _____ .
We discuss matters around the subject but not at the heart of it.	**SYN—, SYM—,** *together, with* When several companies or businessmen join together in order to carry out some large enterprise, such as developing the petroleum resources of a country, they constitute a _____ .
archfiend	**ARCH,** *first, chief* The person who designs and supervises the construction of a building—the chief builder, in short—is the _____ .
carbohydrates	**HYDR,** *water* A power plant that produces electricity by means of water power is called a _____ plant.
philosopher	**PHIL, PHILE,** *love* The root *adelph* means "brother." The American city commonly referred to as the city of brotherly love is _____ .

page 62

defrost

29

DE—, *off, down, the reverse*
A person who feels gloomy and cast down is _____ .
(Either of two different words beginning with DE— will complete this sentence.)

30

All future generations—i.e., those that come after you.

95

POST—, *after*
What part of a creature does the word *posterior* specify?

96

---

commerce

156

COM—, *with, together*
The root *miser* means "to pity." When you express sympathy for someone, you _____ with him.

157

---

decimal

214

CENT, *hundred*
A hundredth part of a dollar is a _____ .

215

When he is too quick to believe things.

280

CRED, *believe, trust*
When we react to a statement with *incredulity*, how do we react?

281

---

superfluous

347

FLU, *flow*
The root *melli* means "honey." When do we call a voice *mellifluous*?

348

He is convicted of wrongdoing in discharging his public duties.

414

MAL, *bad*
When a person who is not definitely sick says that he is suffering from a *malaise*, what does he mean?

page 63

415

posture 481	**POS, PON,** *place, put* Using the prefix DE—, finish this statement: When a person is ousted from a position of power, he is _____.	482
terrain *or* territory 546	**TERR, TERRA, TER,** *earth, land* Angels are celestial beings, but men are _____ creatures.	547
atypical 610	**A—, AN—** (before vowels), *not, without* A drug which permits a person to feel no pain, as in a surgical operation, is called an _____.	611
syndicate 676	**SYN—, SYM—,** *together, with* The place where Jews come together for religious services is called a temple or _____.	677
architect 734	**ARCH,** *first, chief* The study of the first or earliest societies, mainly by excavating and examining their ruins, is called _____.	735
hydroelectric 799	**LEON, LION,** *lion* If, like Stephen A. Douglas or John L. Lewis, a man looks brave and stalwart, perhaps with thick hair swept back like a mane, people say he looks _____.	800
Philadelphia 865	**PHIL, PHILE,** *love* The root *Anglo* means "English." A person who loves the English is an _____.	866

depressed *or* dejected	**DE—**, *off, down, the reverse* The reverse of inflation is _____ .
30	31
The tail end.	**PRE—**, *before* When the parts of something, such as a house, have been *fabricated* before they are fitted together, they have been _____ .
96	97
commiserate	**COM—**, *with, together* The root *mod* means "extent." What kind of room is a *commodious* room?
157	158
cent	**CENT**, *hundred* A hundred years is a _____ .
215	216
We react with disbelief.	**CRED**, *believe, trust* When a rumor or report inspires *credence,* what does it inspire?
281	282
When it flows sweetly, like honey.	**FLU**, *flow* What is the *confluence* of two or more rivers?
348	349
He means he is suffering from a vague feeling of ill-being.	**MATER, MATR**, *mother* Your ancestors on your mother's side are called your _____ ancestors.
415	416

page 65

deposed	**POS, PON,** *place, put* Using the prefix EX—, finish this sentence: A large fair, where exhibits are set out for inspection and entertainment, is often called an _____ .
terrestrial	**TERR, TERRA, TER,** *earth, land* Using the prefix SUB—, finish this statement: A river that flows underground is a _____ river.
anesthetic	**A—, AN—** (before vowels), *not, without* The root *byss* means "bottom." Anything that is so deep that it practically has no bottom—an ocean depth, for instance—is an _____ .
synagogue	**SYN—, SYM—,** *together, with* The root *tax* means "arrange." The way words are arranged, or put together, in a sentence constitutes its _____ .
archeology	**ARCH,** *first, chief* The first version or model of its *type*—the first airplane, for example—is referred to as the _____ .
leonine	**LEON, LION,** *lion* If an individual is feted and acclaimed, especially in fashionable society, he is _____ .
Anglophile	**POLIT, POLIS,** *civic, city, citizen* A person who makes a profession of getting elected to public office is a _____ .

page 66

deflation **31**	**DE—**, *off, down, the reverse* The root *celer* means "swift." When a motorist reduces his speed, he _____ . **32**
prefabricated **97**	**PRE—**, *before* When, in school or college, it is *requisite* that one course be taken before another, the first course is called a _____ . **98**
A room with plenty of space. **158**	**COM—**, *with, together* What do we mean when we say that two people—e.g., a husband and wife—are *compatible*? **159**
century **216**	**CENT**, *hundred* A certain worm-like creature has so many feet that it is called a _____ . **217**
It inspires belief. **282**	**CRED**, *belief, trust* What does an individual do when he sets forth his *credo*? **283**
The place where they flow together. **349**	**FLU**, *flow* What kind of person is an *affluent* person? **350**
maternal **416**	**MATER, MATR**, *mother* A hospital for prospective mothers is known as a _____ hospital. **417**

page 67

exposition

POS, PON, *place, put*
Again using the prefix EX—, complete this sentence: The kind of writing whose purpose is to explain and put things in proper perspective is _____ writing.

subterranean

TERR, TERRA, TER, *earth, land*
Using the prefix IN—, complete this sentence: If you bury something in the earth, especially a dead body, you _____ it.

abyss

A—, AN— (before vowels), *not, without*
The root *damant* means "subdue." An individual who will not yield to pressure is an _____ individual.

syntax

SYN—, SYM—, *together, with*
The root *drome* means "run." The symptoms which go together and characterize a particular disease are known as the _____ of that disease.

archetype

ARCH, *first, chief*
Using the prefix AN—, finish this sentence: When a society has no effective rulers or chiefs, the result is a state of _____ .

lionized

LEON, LION, *lion*
The root *chame* means "on the ground." A lizard, notable for its ability to change color, that resembles a little lion on the ground, is known as a _____ .

politician

POLIT, POLIS, *civic, city, citizen*
The capital city of *Indiana* is _____ .

decelerates	**DE—**, *off, down, the reverse* The root *foli* means "leaf." If you strip the leaves from a tree, you _____ it.
32	33
prerequisite	**PRE—**, *before* If you believe that your destiny has already been determined for you, you believe in _____ .
98	99
They get along well.	NOTE: Like the preceding prefix, COM— is subject to assimilation. Before *l*, it becomes COL—, as in *collide* and *collaborate*. Before *r*, it becomes COR—, as in *correspond* and *correlate*.
159	
centipede	**CENT**, *hundred* The celebration of the one hundredth anniversary of an event is often called the _____ celebration.
217	218
He sets forth his basic beliefs.	**CURR, CUR**, *run, go* The flow of a river is usually referred to as its _____ .
283	284
A prosperous person, one to whom wealth has come.	**FORM**, *form, rule* An individual who always follows the proper rules—in dress, manners, and speech, for instance—is a _____ individual.
350	351
maternity	**MATER, MATR**, *mother* The college that a person has attended is often referred to as his alma _____ .
417	418

page 69

expository 484	**POS, PON**, *place, put* Using the prefix COM—, complete this statement: A part which, along with other parts, makes up a whole—the carburetor in an engine, for example—is a _____ part. 485
inter 549	**TERR, TERRA, TER**, *earth, land* Using the prefixes DIS— and IN—, finish this sentence: If you dig up something that has been buried in the earth, you _____ it. 550
adamant 613	NOTE: Many words begin with A— or AN—. But A— or AN— usually means "not" or "without" only in those words whose roots are also of Greek origin.
syndrome 679	**SYN—, SYM—**, *together, with* What kind of meeting, often held at schools and colleges, is a *symposium*? 680
anarchy 737	**ARCH**, *first, chief* The root *olig* means "few." When only a few individuals rule a group or a society, they are known as an _____ . 738
chameleon 802	**LEON, LION**, *lion* The French name for a common weed with yellow flowers resembling lion's teeth is *dent de lion*. It appears in English as _____ . 803
Indianapolis 868	**POLIT, POLIS**, *civic, city, citizen* The root *minnea*, of Indian origin, means "water." The largest city in Minnesota, a city with many lakes and rivers, is _____ . 869

defoliate	**DE—**, *off, down, the reverse* The root *cid* means "to fall." As distinguished from evergreens, what kind of trees are *deciduous* trees?
33	34
predestination	**PRE—**, *before* Introductory remarks, especially those with which a book begins, are often called a _____ .
99	100
	Before a number of other consonants, unnecessary to specify, it becomes CON—, as in *conform* and *consolidate*. Before a vowel, it becomes CO—, as in *coeducational* and *coeditor*.
centennial	**MILL**, *thousand* A thousandth part of a dollar (one tenth of a cent) is a _____ .
218	219
current	**CURR, CUR**, *run, go* The "run" of courses in a school or college constitutes its _____ .
284	285
formal	**FORM**, *form, rule* The early years of a child's life, when his character is first established, are often called his _____ years.
351	352
mater	**MATER, MATR**, *mother* A married woman, especially if she has children or is no longer in her first youth, is commonly called a _____ .
418	419

page 71

component

485

	POS, PON, *place, put* What kind of picture is a *composite* picture? 486

disinter

550

	Before proceeding to Frame 551, do Review 5 on page 153.

	ANTI—, ANT— (before vowels), *against, opposite* A person who impairs the *social* well-being of other people, or who simply avoids their company, is an _____ individual. 614

One where people come together to exchange views.

680

	Before proceeding to Frame 681, do the Review on page 157.

oligarchy

738

	AUTO, *self* If you write a biography of yourself, you write an _____ . 739

dandelion

803

	LOG(UE), LOGY, *speech, study, collection* The rules and procedures of verbal reasoning, first codified by Aristotle, constitute the science of _____ . 804

Minneapolis

869

	POLIT, POLIS, *civic, city, citizen* The root *metro* means "mother." The chief city in a region—the mother city, as it were—is a _____ . 870

page 72

Those that shed their leaves annually. 34	**DE**, *off, down, the reverse* When property has *depreciated,* what has happened to it? 35
preface 100	**PRE—**, *before* The root *coc,* meaning "to cook," assumes a figurative meaning in the word *precocious.* What is a precocious child? 101
	IN—, *not* If a substance is not edible, it is _____. 160
mill 219	**MILL**, *thousand* A thousand thousand is a _____. 220
curriculum 285	**CURR, CUR**, *run, go* Using the prefix EX—, finish this statement: If you take a short trip for pleasure, you take an _____. 286
formative 352	**FORM**, *form, rule* A fixed rule or method for doing something, as in mathematics or chemistry, is a _____. 353
matron 419	**MATER, MATR**, *mother* One of the meanings of the root *arch* is "ruler." What kind of society is a *matriarchal* society? 420

page 73

One in which several images are combined or put together.

POS, PON, *place, put*
If you are a *proponent* of a cause—prison reform, let us say—what do you do?

TRACT, *draw, pull*
A vehicle used for such things as drawing farm machinery and pulling loads is a _____ .

---

antisocial

ANTI—, ANT— (before vowels), *against, opposite*
A law which forbids the formation of a business monopoly, or *trust,* is an _____ law.

---

7   Greek Suffixes

(Frames 681–690)

---

autobiography

AUTO, *self*
Anything that is self-operating is _____ .

---

logic

LOG(UE), LOGY, *speech, study, collection*
A lecture on a trip, usually illustrated, is a _____ .

---

metropolis

POLIT, POLIS, *civic, city, citizen*
One of the meanings of the root *acro* is "highest." The highest point in Athens, on which the Parthenon was built, is called the _____ .

page 74

It has gone down in value. 35	**DE—**, *off, down, the reverse* What do we do when we *deprecate* a person's achievements? 36
One who develops early. 101	**PRE—**, *before* When, in speaking of a position you hold, you mention your *predecessor,* to whom are you referring? 102
inedible 160	**IN—**, *not* If a statement is not coherent, it is _____. 161
million 220	**MILL**, *thousand* A period of a thousand years is a _____. 221
excursion 286	**CURR, CUR**, *run, go* Using the prefix IN—, complete this statement: An invasion, especially a short, running one, such as a cavalry raid, is an _____. 287
formula 353	**FORM**, *form, rule* Using the prefixes MIS— and IN—, what is another word for *deceive* ? _____ 354
A society ruled by mothers (or women). 420	**MED**, *middle* A man who is neither tall nor short is of _____ height. 421

You put forth or support that cause. 487	Before proceeding to Frame 488, do Review 4 on page 151.
tractor 551	**TRACT,** *draw, pull* Using the prefix DIS—, finish this statement: If you draw a person's attention away from what he is doing, you _____ him. 552
antitrust 615	**ANTI—, ANT—** (before vowels), *against, opposite* The northernmost region of the earth is the *Arctic.* The southernmost region is the _____ . 616
	—ITIS, *inflammation* Inflammation of the *appendix* is _____ ; of the *larynx,* _____ ; of the *bronchial* tubes, _____ . 681
automatic 740	**AUTO,** *self* Whatever is written in a person's own hand, especially his signature, is an _____ . 741
travelogue *or* travelog 805	**LOG(UE), LOGY,** *speech, study, collection* Beginning with MONO, complete this sentence: A long discourse by one person is called, sometimes disparagingly, a _____ . 806
Acropolis 871	**POLIT, POLIS,** *civic, city, citizen* The root *cosmo* means "world." A person of wide international experience, one who feels at home in many countries—a kind of world citizen, in short—is a _____ . 872

We belittle his achievements. 36	NOTE: Occasionally the prefix DE— is simply used to intensify the meaning of the root that follows it, as in *declaim* and *deplore*. Furthermore, it should not be confused with the French word *de*, which means "of," as in *de luxe* and *coup de grâce*.
The person who held the position before you did. 102	**PRO—**, *forth, in front of, instead of* Before the jet age, all airplanes were driven forward by means of _____ . 103
incoherent 161	**IN—**, *not* The root *articul* means "to speak clearly." When a person cannot express his thoughts clearly, we frequently say he is _____ . 162
millennium 221	Before proceeding to Frame 222, do the Review on page 143.
incursion 287	**CURR, CUR**, *run, go* Using the prefix RE—, finish this sentence: A disease that keeps returning is a _____ disease. 288
misinform 354	**FORM**, *form, rule* Using the prefix CON—, what is a word for a person who automatically and unquestioningly obeys all the rules and customs of his group? _____ 355
medium 421	**MED**, *middle* A performance—that of an actor, let us say—which is neither good nor bad is a _____ performance. 422

POTENT, *power*
The abilities which an individual possesses but which have not been developed or realized are his _____ abilities.

488

---

distract

TRACT, *draw, pull*
Using the prefix PRO—, finish this sentence: A long, drawn-out silence is a _____ silence.

552 | 553

Antarctic

ANTI—, ANT— (before vowels), *against, opposite*
When an event does not end after reaching its *climax,* but instead continues on and ends in an undramatic way, we say it ends in an _____.

616 | 617

---

appendicitis, laryngitis, bronchitis

—ITIS, *inflammation*
The root *hepat* means "liver." Inflammation of the liver is _____.

681 | 682

---

autograph

AUTO, *self*
The root *nomy* means "law." To the extent that a town or county can make its own laws without interference from the state or national government, it enjoys local _____.

741 | 742

---

monologue *or* monolog

LOG(UE), LOGY, *speech, study, collection*
The root *zoo* means "animal." The science devoted to the study of animals is called _____.

806 | 807

---

cosmopolite *or* cosmopolitan

POLY, *many*
Words of many *syllables* are described as _____.

872 | *page 78* | 873

DEMI—, *half, less than usual*
In mythology, the offspring of a god and a human being is a _____

37

propellers

PRO—, *forth, in front of, instead of*
A person who stands out, or in front of others—a leader, for instance—is a _____ person.

103 104

inarticulate

IN—, *not*
The root *clement* means "merciful." Severe weather is often called _____ weather.

162 163

5 Latin Roots

(Frames 222–608)

recurrent *or* recurring

CURR, CUR, *run, go*
What do we mean when we say that Judaism was the *precursor* of Christianity?

288 289

conformist

FORM, *form, rule*
Again using the prefix RE—, finish this sentence: In the sixteenth century, Martin Luther began the movement which became known as the Protestant _____ .

355 356

mediocre

MED, *middle*
The great sea between Europe and Africa is the _____ .

422

page 79

423

potential

488

POTENT, *power*
A ruler or other powerful person is sometimes called a _____.

489

---

protracted

553

TRACT, *draw, pull*
When, having erred, a newspaper prints a *retraction,* what does it print?

554

---

anticlimax

617

ANTI—, ANT— (before vowels), *against, opposite*
The root *dote* means "given." Anything given against a poison or any other evil is an _____.

618

---

hepatitis

682

—OID, *resembling, like*
Whatever resembles a *sphere* is _____.

683

---

autonomy

742

AUTO, *self*
The root *crat* means "rule." A ruler who answers only to himself for what he does is an _____.

743

---

zoology

807

LOG(UE), LOGY, *speech, study, collection*
The root *ornitho* means "bird." The science devoted to the study of birds is called _____.

808

---

polysyllabic

873

POLY, *many*
An individual who speaks two languages is *bilingual.* One who speaks many languages is _____.

page 80

874

demigod	**DEMI—**, *half, less than usual* The French word *tasse* means "cup." A small cup of black after-dinner coffee is a _____ .
prominent	**PRO—**, *forth, in front of, instead of* Words such as *he, she,* and *it,* which are used instead of nouns, are called _____ .
inclement	NOTE: Before *l*, IN— usually becomes IL—, as in *illegal* and *illegible*. Before *r*, IN— usually becomes IR—, as in *irresponsible* and *irreligious*. Before *m* or *p*, IN— usually becomes IM—, as in *immobile* and *impossible*.
	ALI, *other, another* If an individual can produce evidence that he was not present when a crime was committed, he has an _____ .
We mean Judaism was the forerunner of Christianity.	**CURR, CUR**, *run, go* When a person is convicted on several counts, each carrying a separate sentence, and the judge decides that the sentences shall be served *concurrently*, what has the judge decided?
Reformation	**FORM**, *form, rule* What is the *format* of a book or magazine?
Mediterranean	**MED**, *middle* We call the period between the fall of the Roman Empire and the beginning of the Renaissance the Middle Ages, or the _____ period.

potentate 489	**POTENT,** *power* What is a word using the prefix IM— that means *powerless*? _____ 490
It prints a statement withdrawing something it has previously printed. 554	**TRACT,** *draw, pull* What kind of individual is an *intractable* individual? 555
antidote 618	**ANTI—, ANT—** (before vowels), *against, opposite* The root *agon* means "contest." Anyone who fights, or contends, with you is your _____ . 619
spheroid 683	**—OID,** *resembling, like* A disease which resembles *rheumatism* is a _____ disease. 684
autocrat 743	**BIO,** *life* The science of life is called _____ . 744
ornithology 808	**LOG(UE), LOGY,** *speech, study, collection* The root *ideo* means "idea." The collection of ideas or doctrines which characterizes a person or group constitutes that person's or that group's _____ . 809
polylingual *or* polyglot 874	**POLY,** *many* The custom which permits a woman to have more than one husband at a time, as in Tibet, is known as _____ . 875

page 82

demitasse	**DIS—**, *opposite of, away from* The opposite of *enchant* is _____.
pronouns	**PRO—**, *forth, in front of, instead of* One of the meanings of the root *log(ue)* is "speech." An introductory speech before a play begins is a _____.
	But the prefix IN—, sometimes from Latin and sometimes from Old English, also means simply "in," as in *insert* and *inbred*. The sense of "in" is also conveyed by IM—, EN—, and EM— (from Latin, Greek, or both), as in *implant*, *energy*, and *embroil*.
alibi	**ALI**, *other, another* An assumed name, such as people in the underworld often use, is known as an _____.
He has decided the sentences shall run at the same time (instead of one after the other).	**CURR, CUR**, *run, go* When we read a book in a *cursory* fashion, how do we read it?
Its general make-up—its size, binding, paper, etc.	**FORM**, *form, rule* When we do something *pro forma*—something we may not take seriously or especially believe in—why do we do it?
medieval	**MED**, *middle* An individual who acts as a go-between or peacemaker for parties in dispute is called a *mediator* or, using the prefix INTER—, an _____.

page 83

impotent

POTENT, *power*
The root *omni* means "all." A synonym for *all-powerful* is
_____ .

One who is stubborn, not easily led.

TRIBUT, *give*
A gift, a speech, or a ceremony which honors or expresses respect for someone is a _____ to him.

---

antagonist

APO—, *away from*
The mark of punctuation which indicates that one or more letters have been removed from a word is the _____ .

---

rheumatoid

—OID, *resembling, like*
The root *aden* means "gland." The lumps of tissue in the pharynx that look like glands are called _____ .

---

biology

BIO, *life*
James Boswell's life of Samuel Johnson is a famous _____ .

---

ideology

LOG(UE), LOGY, *speech, study, collection*
The root *techno* means "skill." The collection of practical skills employed in an industry make up the _____ of that industry.

---

polyandry

POLY, *many*
The root *nes* means "island." The collective name for a numerous group of islands which includes Hawaii, Samoa, and Tahiti is
_____ .

disenchant 39	**DIS—**, *opposite of, away from* If something is jarred away from its regular location, such as a muscle in a sprained shoulder, it is _____. (Either of two different words beginning with DIS— will complete this sentence.) 40
prologue *or* prolog 106	**PRO—**, *forth, in front of, instead of* The root *ject* means "to throw." Anything designed to be thrown forward—e.g., a shell or rocket—is a _____. 107
	SUB—, *under, less* A warship that can operate under water is called a _____. 164
alias 223	**ALI**, *other, another* A person who lives in one country but is a citizen of another country is legally designated as an _____. 224
We read it hastily and superficially—we run through it. 291	Before proceeding to Frame 292, do Review 1 on page 145.
We do it for the sake of form. 358	**GRAD, GRESS**, *go, step* If you proceed step by step towards a goal, instead of by leaps and bounds, you proceed _____. 359
intermediary (or, less commonly, intermediator) 425	Before proceeding to Frame 426, do Review 3 on page 149.

page 85

omnipotent

491

POTENT, *power*
The root *pleni* means "full." An ambassador with full authority to negotiate on behalf of his country is called a _____.

492

tribute

556

TRIBUT, *give*
A river that flows into a larger river is a _____.

557

apostrophe

620

APO—, *away from*
The disciples Christ sent away to preach the Gospel are called the _____.

621

adenoids

685

—OID, *resembling, like*
The root *ov* means "egg." Anything shaped like an egg can be described as oval, or _____.

686

biography

745

BIO, *life*
The name for that science which deals with the *chemistry* of living organisms is _____.

746

technology

810

MEGA, MEGALO, *large, great*
A funnel-shaped instrument for amplifying sound is a _____.

811

Polynesia

876

POLY, *many*
Why are certain schools called *polytechnic* schools?

page 86

877

dislocated *or* displaced	**DIS—**, *opposite of, away from* An individual who believes that nations should reduce or eliminate their armaments believes in _____ .	
40		41
projectile	**PRO—**, *forth, in front of, instead of* The root *lix* means "to flow." What do we mean when we speak of a writer or speaker as *prolix*?	
107		108
submarine	**SUB—**, *under, less* A creature who is less than human is _____ .	
164		165
alien	**ALI**, *other, another* Using the prefix IN—, finish this sentence: Individual rights which cannot be taken away or given to another person—such as those guaranteed in the Constitution—are called _____ .	
224		225
	DICT, *say* When a stenographer, at your direction, writes down what you say, she takes your _____ .	
		292
gradually	**GRAD, GRESS**, *go, step* Using the prefix CON—, what is the word that designates the legislature of the United States? _____	
359		360
	MEMOR, *memory* Ceremonies that honor and perpetuate the memory of a person or an event are _____ ceremonies.	
	page 87	426

plenipotentiary	**PRIM**, *first* An elementary textbook, especially in grade school, is a _____.
tributary	**TRIBUT**, *give* Using the prefix AT—, what is another word for *assign* or *ascribe*? _____
Apostles	**APO—**, *away from* The root *gee* (a variant form of *geo*) means "earth." When, in making its revolutions, the moon—or any other satellite, such as a space ship—is furthest from the earth, it is at its _____.
ovoid	**—OSIS**, *condition* (usually a sick condition) The root *neur* means "nerve." A nervous or emotional disorder is commonly referred to as a _____.
biochemistry	**BIO**, *life* The branch of *physics* that deals with living organisms is called _____.
megaphone	**MEGA, MEGALO**, *large, great* An individual afflicted with delusions of or a *mania* for grandeur is suffering from _____.
Because they specialize in many technical and scientific subjects.	**PROTO**, *first, fundamental* The first version or model of its *type* is called the *archetype* or the _____.

page 88

disarmament

DIS—, *opposite of, away from*
The root *tend* means "to stretch." If something is stretched out of place, such as a swollen belly, it is _____ .

41 42

He is wordy and long-winded.

PRO—, *forth, in front of, instead of*
Why are certain authors, such as Charles Dickens and Sinclair Lewis, called *prolific* authors?

108 109

subhuman

SUB—, *under, less*
The root *jug* means "a yoke." If you conquer things—e.g., other countries or your passions—you _____ them.

165 166

inalienable

ALI, *other, another*
When the affections of a woman who is attached to a man are *alienated* by another man, what happens to the affections?

225 226

dictation

DICT, *say*
A person's way of expressing himself orally, including his choice of words and his enunciation, is called his _____ .

292 293

Congress

GRAD, GRESS, *go, step*
Using the prefix DE—, finish this statement: If you bring a person into disrepute or contempt, you _____ him.

360 361

memorial *or* commemorative

MEMOR, *memory*
A note written to aid the memory, or a written communication between offices in a business or governmental organization is a _____ .

426 *page 89* 427

primer	**PRIM,** *first* The leading female performer in an opera company is called the _____ donna.	
493		494
attribute	**TRIBUT,** *give* Using the prefix RE—, finish this sentence: Punishment or repayment for wrongdoing is called _____ .	
558		559
apogee	**APO—,** *away from* When a person is accused of being an *apostate,* what is he accused of?	
622		623
neurosis	**—OSIS,** *condition* (usually a sick condition) The root *thromb* means "a clot." A blood clot that impedes circulation is called a _____ .	
687		688
biophysics	**BIO,** *life* Using the prefix ANTI—, finish this sentence: Certain substances which act against bacteria—e.g., penicillin and the sulfa drugs—are known as _____ .	
747		748
megalomania	**MEGA, MAGALO,** *large, great* In the metric system, *mega* (*meg* before a vowel) means one million, as in *megameter, megacycle,* and *megohm.* Thus, an explosive force equal to a million *tons* of TNT is a _____ .	
812		813
prototype	**PROTO,** *first, fundamental* All one-celled creatures, belonging to the most primitive division of the animal kingdom—amoebas, for example—are called _____ .	
878	page 90	879

distended	**DIS—**, *opposite of, away from* The root *sip* means "to throw." If you squander your resources, you _____ them.
42	43
Because they produced, or brought forth, many works.	NOTE: The prefix PRO— also means *in favor of,* as in pro-American, pro-English, prolabor, etc.
109	
subjugate	**SUB—**, *under, less* The Latin word *poena* means "penalty." A writ which orders a person to appear in court, under penalty of the law if he disregards it, is called a _____ .
166	167
They are transferred to the other man.	**ALTER**, *other, another* When you change anything into another form, you make _____ in it.
226	227
diction	**DICT**, *say* Using the prefix E—, what is another word for *decree* or *proclamation*? _____
293	294
degrade	**GRAD, GRESS**, *go, step* Using the prefix AG—, complete this sentence: A person who is quick to take action, perhaps at the expense of others, is an _____ person.
361	362
memorandum	**MEMOR**, *memory* Autobiographies and other writings based on the recollection of personal experience are sometimes called _____ .
427	428

page 91

prima 494	**PRIM**, *first* The evidence against an accused person which, at the first judicial examination of it, is sufficient to hold the person for trial is _____ facie evidence. 495
retribution 559	**VAG**, *wander* The legal term for a tramp is _____ . 560
He is accused of having abandoned some faith, cause, or party. 623	**CATA—**, *down* A book or pamphlet in which items are listed, or written down, is a _____ . 624
thrombosis 688	**—OSIS**, *condition* (usually a sick condition) The root *hypn* means "sleep." The psychic inducement of a kind of trance or sleep is known as _____ . 689
antibiotics 748	**BIO**, *life* Using the prefix SYM—, finish this statement: If two species live together to the detriment of one, the relationship is parasitical. If they live together to their mutual advantage, the relationship is _____ . 749
megaton 813	**MICRO**, *small* The small *grooves* in long-playing records are called _____ . 814
protozoans *or* protozoa 879	**PROTO**, *first, fundamental* A matter of etiquette or precedence—of who comes first, as it were—especially in diplomatic and military circles, is a matter of _____ . 880

page 92

dissipate

DIS—, *opposite of, away from*
The root *semin* means "to sow." What do you do when you *disseminate* your ideas?

QUASI—, *largely, almost, seemingly*
Alleged events for which there is some *historical* evidence but not enough to prove their occurrence beyond question are called _____ events.

subpoena

SUB—, *under, less*
The root *sid* means "to sit." What kind of company is a *subsidiary* company?

alterations

ALTER, *other, another*
If a person is compelled to act in a certain way, we frequently say that he has no _____ .

edict

DICT, *say*
The root *bene* means "good." A blessing, especially in church services, is often called a _____ .

aggressive

GRAD, GRESS, *go, step*
Using the prefix DI— (a variant form of DIS—), complete this statement: In speaking or writing, a departure from the main subject is a _____ .

memoirs

MEMOR, *memory*
Using the prefix IM—, finish this sentence: Anything that is so ancient—e.g., the custom of marriage—that it reaches back into times beyond memory or historical record is

_____ .

page 93

prima 495	**PRIM**, *first* The law of inheritance whereby land descends exclusively to the first son, long the rule in England but abolished in America after the American Revolution, is known as the law of _____. 496
vagrant 560	**VAG**, *wander* A more romantic word for an idle man who wanders from place to place is _____. 561
catalogue 624	**CATA—**, *down* The sudden and general downfall of an important enterprise is a _____. 625
hypnosis 689	**—OSIS**, *condition* (usually a sick condition) The root *scler* means "hard." What is *arteriosclerosis*? 690
symbiotic 749	**CHRON**, *time* A symptom which persists or recurs over a long period of time is a _____ symptom. 750
microgrooves 814	**MICRO**, *small* The *film* on which books and documents are photographed in reduced size is called _____. 815
protocol 880	**PROTO**, *first, fundamental* The fundamental substance in all animal and plant cells is _____. 881

You spread them abroad. 44	**DIS—**, *opposite of, away from* What kind of person is a *disconsolate* person? 45
quasi-historical 110	**QUASI—**, *largely, almost, seemingly* Government boards which are not courts but which subpoena witnesses, hold hearings, and perform other *judicial* functions are _____ boards. 111
One controlled by another company. 168	**SUB—**, *under, less* What do we mean when we say that someone is *subservient*? 169
alternative 228	**ALTER**, *other, another* When you do something every other day, you do it on _____ days. 229
benediction 295	**DICT**, *say* The root *male* means "evil." The opposite of a blessing is a curse, or _____ . 296
digression 363	Before proceeding to Frame 364, do Review 2 on page 147.
immemorial 429	**MEMOR**, *memory* What do we mean when we say an event is *memorable*? 430

page 95

primogeniture 496	**PRIM**, *first* In botany and zoology, why are certain species of plants and animals, often extinct, referred to as *primitive, primeval,* or *primordial*? 497
vagabond 561	**VAG**, *wander* Using the prefix EXTRA—, finish this statement: A lavish or spectacular theatrical production, especially if it is a musical show, is often advertised as an _____. 562
catastrophe 625	**CATA—**, *down* Why are certain cemeteries in Rome, in some of which early Christians took refuge, called *catacombs*? 626
A hardening of the arteries. 690	**8 Greek Numbers** (Frames 691–725)
chronic 750	**CHRON**, *time* If events are listed in the order of their occurrence, they are listed in _____ order. 751
microfilm 815	**MICRO**, *small* A tiny living organism, especially a germ that causes disease, is a _____. 816
protoplasm 881	**PROTO**, *first, fundamental* One of the fundamental particles in the atom, along with the electron, the neutron, and so on, is the _____. 882

page 96

One who cannot be consoled. 45	**EX—, E—,** *out* A doorway leading out, as in a theatre, is an _____. 46
quasi-judicial 111	NOTE: When QUASI— is used as a prefix it is attached, usually with a hyphen, to full-fledged words, as in *quasi-professional* and *quasi-religious*. But commonly it appears as a separate word, as in *quasi alliance* and *quasi painful*. Furthermore, its meaning is ambiguous and
He serves under authority in a docile and obedient way. 169	NOTE: This prefix is also subject to assimilation, as in *succumb, suppress,* and *surreptitious.* Consequently, if you encounter a word that begins with SU- plus a double consonant, the chances are you are dealing with a variant form of SUB—.
alternate 229	**ALTER,** *other, another* If an individual gets into an angry dispute with another person, he gets into an _____ with him. 230
malediction 296	**DICT,** *say* The Latin word *vale* means "farewell." The student who delivers the farewell speech at graduation ceremonies is called the _____. 297
	GRAN, *grain, seed* A barn for storing grain is a _____. 364
We mean it is a notable event worth remembering. 430	**ORDIN, ORDAIN,** *order* A regulation enacted by a city government is usually called a local _____. 431

page 97

Because they were the first of their kind to appear.	**PRIM**, *first* Why is the Archbishop of Canterbury called the *primate* of the Church of England?
497	498
extravaganza	**VAG**, *wander* What do we mean when we say of an eccentric individual that he is subject to *vagaries*?
562	563
Because they are underground.	**CATA—**, *down* When we refer to the *cataclysms* of nature, what are we referring to?
626	627
	MONO, *one* A word of one *syllable* is called a _____ .
	691
chronological	**CHRON**, *time* A history, especially one in which events are recorded simply in the order in which they occurred, without comment or interpretation, is also called a _____ .
751	752
microbe *or* microorganism	**MICRO**, *small* The branch of *biology* that studies such organisms is known as _____ .
816	817
proton	**PROTO**, *first, fundamental* In a play or story, who is the *protagonist*?
882	883

exit

46

EX–, E–, *out*
A species that has died out is an _____ species.

47

---

must be inferred from its context. *Quasi-professional* might mean seemingly professional but perhaps not actually, thus suggesting the possibility of deception or superficiality, or it might mean almost or largely professional in all truth.

Before proceeding to the Latin suffixes that follow on this band, do Review 3 on page 141.

---

altercation

ALTER, *other, another*
Under what circumstances does a person deserve to be called *altruistic*?

230

231

---

valedictorian

DICT, *say*
The root *juris* means "law." The area within which a court must be heeded in the matter of hearing and deciding cases constitutes the court's _____ .

297

298

---

granary

GRAN, *grain, seed*
A hard stone, used for building and grained like wood, is called _____ .

364

365

---

ordinance

ORDIN, ORDAIN, *order*
Numbers which express order—*first, second, third,* etc., as distinguished from *one, two, three,* etc.—are known as _____ numbers.

431

page 99

432

Because he ranks above all other bishops in his church. 498	**PRIM**, *first* In biology, why are man, the apes, and certain other mammals assigned to the order of *Primates*? 499
We mean his conduct is sometimes odd or capricious. 563	**VEN**, *come, go* If you set out on some risky errand or mission, you _____ forth. 564
To great, violent occurrences—floods, earthquakes, etc. 627	**DIA—**, *across, through* A straight line through the center of a circle represents the circle's _____. 628
monosyllable 691	**MONO**, *one* If an individual speaks in the same unvarying *tone*, he speaks in a _____. 692
chronicle 752	**CHRON**, *time* The root *meter* means "measure." Another word for *clock*, especially for the highly accurate kind used on ships, is _____. 753
microbiology 817	**MICRO**, *small* The root *nes* means "island." The collective name for a group of small islands in the western Pacific, a group which includes the Carolines, Marshalls, and Marianas, is _____. 818
The hero—i.e., the chief, or first, character. 883	**SCOP**, *see* If a man's range of knowledge or understanding is small, we say he is a man of narrow _____. 884

page 100

extinct

47

EX—, E—, *out*
The word that describes the escape of water in the form of *vapor* from some substance is _____ .

48

RE—, *again, back*
When you construct something again, you _____ it.

112

3 Latin Suffixes

(Frames 170–181)

When he devotes himself to the welfare of others.

231

ALTER, *other, another*
The Latin word *ego* means "I." What does an individual mean when he refers to another person as his *alter ego*?

232

jurisdiction

298

EQUI, EQUA, *equal*
Two things that are equal in value are _____ to one another.

299

granite

365

GRAN, *grain, seed*
Anything reduced to small particles, as sugar and salt usually are, has been _____ .

366

ordinal

432

ORDIN, ORDAIN, *order*
When an individual is made a clergyman—when, in other words, he receives holy orders—he is said to be _____ .

433

Because they are the most highly evolved mammals. 499	**RUPT,** *break* An appropriate word for a break in various things, from diplomatic relations to man's internal organs, is _____ . 500
venture 564	**VEN,** *come, go* Using the prefix CON—, complete this sentence: The place where nuns have come together in order to live a religious life is a _____ . 565
diameter 628	**DIA—,** *across, through* A conversation between two or more people is a _____ . 629
monotone 692	**MONO,** *one* An airplane with a single spread of wings is a _____ . 693
chronometer 753	**CHRON,** *time* Using the prefix SYN—, complete this sentence: When actions have been timed to occur together—e.g., air and ground actions in a battle—we say they have been _____ . 754
Micronesia 818	**MICRO,** *small* The universe as a whole is sometimes called the *macrocosm*. What do we mean when we refer to man as a *microcosm*? 819
scope 884	**SCOP,** *see* Using the prefix PERI—, finish this statement: The instrument that men in a submarine use for looking around above water is the _____ . 885

page 102

evaporation

EX—, E—, *out*
The opposite of *inject* is _____.

---

reconstruct

RE—, *again, back*
One or more lines that recur at regular intervals in a song or poem are called a _____.

Unlike prefixes, suffixes serve grammatical purposes. They indicate tense, for instance, as in walk*ed*. They indicate gender, or sex, as in actr*ess*. And it is often by means of suffixes that we show that a word is a noun (creat*ion*, plum*age*, happ*iness*, vulgar*ity*), an adjective (cred*ible*, prim*ary*, miracul*ous*, intention*al*), a verb (activ*ate*, glori*fy*, ion*ize*), or an adverb (swift*ly*, sea*ward*).

English makes use of many suffixes from Latin, and also from Greek, but we know most of them so

---

He means the other person is such a close friend that he is like another self.

AM, *love, friend*
A person who does something—plays tennis, let us say—simply because he likes to rather than for pay is an _____.

---

equivalent

EQUI, EQUA, *equal*
The imaginary line that divides the earth into two equal parts is the _____.

---

granulated

GRAN, *grain, seed*
Animals that eat plants are called *herbivorous.* Those that feed on flesh are called *carnivorous.* Those that feed on grain and seeds, such as certain birds, are called _____.

---

ordained

ORDIN, ORDAIN, *order*
Using the prefix PRE—, complete this statement: So many things happen to us unexpectedly that sometimes our lives seem _____ by some higher power.

page 103

rupture 500	**RUPT**, *break* Using the prefix INTER—, finish this statement: If you break into a conversation, you _____ it. 501
convent 565	**VEN**, *come, go* Using the prefix INTER—, finish this sentence: The time between two events is the _____ time. 566
dialogue *or* dialog 629	**DIA**—, *across, through* When a person tries to see through and understand a problem, such as a doctor does with a patient, he is trying to _____ the problem. 630
monoplane 693	**MONO**, *one* An eyeglass for one eye is a _____ . 694
synchronized 754	**CHRON**, *time* The prefix *ana*— means "back." Anything historically out of place, but especially a throwback to a previous era, is an _____ . 755
We mean that man is, within himself, a miniature universe. 819	**MICRO**, *small* In the metric system, *micro* means one millionth. A millionth of a *gram*, therefore, is a _____ . 820
periscope 885	**SCOP**, *see* Using the prefix EPI—, complete this statement: A church, especially a Protestant church, which is governed, or overseen, by bishops is called an _____ church. 886

eject	**EX—, E—,** *out* The root *lucid* means "light." If you clarify a subject—i.e., bring it out into the light—you _____ it.
refrain	**RE—,** *again, back* The root *nov* means "new." When you repair or make something like new again—e.g., the house you live in—you _____ it.
	well that they come to us automatically. The exercises on Latin suffixes which follow, and those on Greek suffixes which we shall encounter later, are confined to a few which, in at least some of their uses, are not so well known.
amateur	**AM,** *love, friend* A love affair, particularly a secret one, is often called an _____ .
equator	**EQUI, EQUA,** *equal* Tightrope walkers must develop a fine sense of _____ .
granivorous	**GRAN,** *grain, seed* The root *pome* means "apple." The name of a red, apple-like fruit which is full of seeds is _____ .
preordained	**ORDIN, ORDAIN,** *order* What is a word using the prefix EXTRA— that means *very unusual*? _____

page 105

interrupt	**RUPT,** *break* Using the prefix DIS—, finish this sentence: When you create disorder at a meeting, you _____ the meeting.
501	502
intervening	**VEN,** *come, go* When a lawyer, feeling that the court in a particular locality may be prejudiced, secures for his client a change of *venue,* what does he secure?
566	567
diagnose	**DIA—,** *across, through* A crown is also called a _____.
630	631
monocle	**MONO,** *one* Any person or group that has exclusive control of something enjoys a _____.
694	695
anachronism	**CYCL,** *circle* A storm in which winds rotate violently is a _____.
755	756
microgram	**MORPH,** *form* The Greek god of dreams, the creator of nocturnal forms and fantasies, was _____.
820	821
episcopal *or* episcopalian	**SCOP,** *see* Using a word beginning with MICRO, finish this sentence: A device for examining very small objects is called a _____.

page 106

elucidate

EX—, E—, *out*
The root *culp* means "fault." When you *exculpate* an accused person, what do you do for him?

---

renovate

RE—, *again, back*
The root *sil* means "to jump." Whatever springs back easily into shape, including a person who recovers quickly from a setback, is _____.

—ANA, —IANA, *items belonging to*
This suffix, usually attached to a proper name, as in *Lincolniana*, designates a collection of miscellaneous and usually minor items concerning a person or place, as distinguished from a systematic biographical or historical presentation. Thus, museums in *America* often contain collections of early _____.

---

amour

AM, *love, friend*
Love adventures are commonly referred to as _____ adventures. (Either of two words beginning with AM will complete this sentence.)

---

equilibrium

EQUI, EQUA, *equal*
If two places are the same distance from where you live, they are _____ from your home.

---

pomegranate

GRAND, *great*
Greatness of really impressive proportions, such as that which is commonly attributed to the Roman Empire, is called _____.

---

extraordinary

ORDIN, ORDAIN, *order*
Using the prefix SUB—, finish this sentence: A person who is below you in rank or under your orders is your _____.

page 107

disrupt	**RUPT,** *break* Using the prefix AB—, what is another word for *sudden* or *brusque*? _____ .
He secures another locality in which to try the case.	**VER,** *true* In judging a case, a judge or jury is supposed to reach a true and valid decision. That is why the decision is called a _____ .
diadem	**DIA—,** *across, through* The root *gon* means "angle" or "corner." A line that slants from one corner to another is a _____ line.
monopoly	**MONO,** *one* The name of a deadly gas which consists of one part carbon and one part oxygen is carbon _____ .
cyclone	**CYCL,** *circle* The recurring circle of events that characterizes an economic system—prosperity, rising prices, depression, falling prices, etc.—is commonly referred to as the business _____ .
Morpheus	**MORPH,** *form* A drug used to relieve pain and induce sleep, whose name was derived from the name of this god, is _____ .
microscope	**SCOP,** *see* The root *tele* means "far off." The instrument for seeing far-off things is the _____ .

page 108

You free him from blame.	**EX–, E–,** *out* The root *radic* means "root." What happens when something is *eradicated*?
51	52
resilient	**RE–,** *again, back* The root *juven* means "young." How does an individual feel when he feels *rejuvenated*?
115	116
Americana	**–ANA, –IANA,** *items belonging to* A collection of sayings, anecdotes, letters and such concerning Thomas *Jefferson* is called _____; concerning Samuel *Johnson*, _____; concerning Ralph Waldo *Emerson*, _____.
170	171
amorous *or* amatory	**AM,** *love, friend* A friendly individual who is likable is an _____ individual.
235	236
equidistant	**EQUI, EQUA,** *equal* Using the prefix AD–, finish this sentence: Whatever is equal to the demands of a situation—e.g., a sum of money—is _____.
302	303
grandeur	**GRAND,** *great* Schemes that are merely pompous, their greatness superficial and unrealistic, are _____ schemes.
369	370
subordinate	**ORDIN, ORDAIN,** *order* What is a word using both the prefixes IN– and SUB– that describes a person who refuses to obey orders? _____
436	437

page 109

abrupt 503	**RUPT**, *break* Using the prefix E—, complete this statement: When lava bursts out of a volcano, we say that the volcano is in _____. 504
verdict 568	**VER**, *true* If you check up on an assertion and substantiate the truth of it, you _____ the assertion. 569
diagonal 632	**DIA—**, *across, through* The root *phragm* means "fence." The partition in the human body which stretches between the chest and the abdomen is the _____. 633
monoxide 696	**MONO**, *one* An individual whose mind is fixed on a single idea is suffering from _____. 697
cycle 757	**CYCL**, *circle* The root *ops* means "eye." In Greek mythology, a member of a race of giants with one round eye in the middle of the forehead was called a _____. 758
morphine 822	**MORPH**, *form* The study of form and structure, whether of words, of geological formations, or of living organisms, is called _____. 823
telescope 888	**SCOP**, *see* The root *horo* means "hour." In astrology, the position of the stars and planets at the hour of your birth determines your _____. 889

page 110

It is wiped, or rooted, out. 52	**EX–, E–,** *out* The root *oner* means "burden." What does a court do when it *exonerates* a defendant? 53
He feels young again. 116	**RE–,** *again, back* The root *gurgit* means "to flood." What occurs when something is *regurgitated*? 117
Jeffersoniana, Johnsoniana, Emersoniana 171	**–ESE,** *belonging to* Whatever belongs to *Portugal*, including its inhabitants and its language, is _____ ; to *Malta*, _____ ; to *Canton*, _____ . 172
amiable 236	**AM,** *love, friend* If you enjoy friendly and peaceable relations with someone, you enjoy _____ relations with him. 237
adequate 303	**EQUI, EQUA,** *equal* The root *anim* means "feeling" or "disposition." If an individual usually maintains an even temper, especially in the face of trouble, he becomes known for his _____ . 304
grandiose 370	**GRAND,** *great* In Spain and Portugal, a nobleman of the highest rank is a _____ . 371
insubordinate 437	**ORDIN, ORDAIN,** *order* What is meant when an individual's desires or ambitions are described as *inordinate*? 438

page 111

eruption

SENS, SENT, *feel, think*
An event that arouses intense interest and excited feelings is a _____ event.

---

verify

VER, *true*
When you doubt an individual's *veracity*, what do you doubt?

---

diaphragm

DIA—, *across, through*
The root *phan* means "to show." Why is gauze-like material commonly described as *diaphanous*?

---

monomania

DI, *two*
If you cannot choose between two alternatives, you are in a _____.

Cyclops

CYCL, *circle*
Using the prefix EN—, finish this sentence: A papal letter of instruction which circulates among the Roman Catholic clergy is known as an _____ letter.

---

morphology

MORPH, *form*
Using the prefix A—, finish this sentence: Anything with no definite form or shape, from an amoeba to the character of a man without convictions, is _____.

---

horoscope

SCOP, *see*
The root *stetho* means "chest." The instrument a doctor uses to listen to sounds in your chest and thus "see" what is going on in it is the _____.

page 112

It acquits him. 53	**EX–, E–,** *out* How do you feel when you feel *enervated*? 54
It flows back, as when one vomits. 117	**RE–,** *again, back* What do you do when you *reiterate* a statement? 118
Portuguese, Maltese, Cantonese 172	**–ESE,** *belonging to* When this suffix is used to designate the language peculiar to a particular occupational group, its effect is usually derogatory. Thus, the jargon of *journalists* is called _____; that of bureaucratic *officials*, _____; that of *business*men, _____. 173
amicable 237	**AM,** *love, friend* What do we mean when we assert that two nations—the United States and Canada, for instance—live in *amity*? 238
equanimity 304	**EQUI, EQUA,** *equal* The Latin word *nox* means "night." What are the vernal and autumnal *equinoxes*? (The first occurs about March 21, the second about September 21.) 305
grandee 371	**GRAND,** *great* The root *loq* means "to speak." What do we mean when we say that someone's manner of speaking is *grandiloquent*? 372
His desires or ambitions are excessive. 438	**PAR,** *equal* Government-supported prices for farm products, calculated to keep the farmer's purchasing power equal to what it once was, are called _____ prices. 439

sensational 505	**SENS, SENT,** *feel, think* An individual devoted to gratifying his bodily or sexual appetites is a _____ individual. 506
You doubt his truthfulness. 570	**VER,** *true* What do we mean when we declare that someone is a *veritable* rascal? 571
Because whatever it covers shows through. 634	**DIA—,** *across, through* The root *spor* means "scatter." When we speak of the Jews in the *Diaspora*, what Jews are we speaking of? 635
dilemma 698	**DI—,** *two* Soda water bubbles because it is charged with a gas which consists of one part carbon for every two parts of oxygen. This gas is called carbon _____ . 699
encyclical 759	**CYCL,** *circle* Again using the prefix EN—, what is the word that designates a volume, or a set of volumes, that encompasses the entire range of knowledge concerning one or more subjects? _____ . 760
amorphous 824	**MORPH,** *form* One of the meanings of the prefix *meta* is "altered." If something alters its form or nature, such as a butterfly when it is ready to leave the cocoon, it undergoes a _____ . 825
stethoscope 890	**THE,** *god* A first name for a man that means "gift of God" is _____ . *page 114* 891

You feel tired out. 54	**EXTRA—**, *beyond, outside* Anything that is beyond the *ordinary* is _____. 55
You repeat it. 118	**RETRO—**, *backward, behind* The *rockets* used to slow down a space vehicle are called _____. 119
journalese, officialese, businessese 173	**—ESQUE**, *in the style of, like* If a woman's figure is tall and shapely, suggesting a *statue*, we say it is _____ . 174
We mean they live in peace and friendship. 238	**ANIM**, *feeling, disposition* Any living being that is not a plant belongs to the _____ kingdom. 239
Those times when the night is equal in length to the day everywhere on earth. 305	**EQUI, EQUA**, *equal* If a region has an *equable* climate, what kind of climate does it have? 306
We mean that it is lofty and high-flown. 372	**GRAND**, *great* When an individual is devoted to *self-aggrandizement*, what is he devoted to? 373
parity 439	**PAR**, *equal* Using the prefix COM—, complete this sentence: things that are about equal, or at least possess similar characteristics, are _____ . 440

page 115

sensual	**SENS, SENT,** *feel, think* A person devoted to gratifying his senses in more refined ways—who especially enjoys beauty and delicacy—is a _____ person.
We mean he is really and truly a rascal.	**VER,** *true* The word *verily,* now archaic, occurs often in early English works, such as the King James version of the Bible. What does the word mean?
Those scattered through the world (not those in Israel).	**EPI—,** *on, upon, to* A nervous disorder in which the victim is seized by fits is called _____ .
dioxide	**DI—,** *two* The root *phthong* means "sound." The sound you make in pronouncing two different vowels in the same syllable—as in the word *house*—is called a _____ .
encyclopedia	**CYCL,** *circle* One of the machines physicists use in studying subatomic particles is the *cyclotron.* What is the first thing this machine does to these particles?
metamorphosis	**MORPH,** *form* Beginning with the root *anthrop(o)* complete this sentence: If you conceive of God in the form of a man, as the Greeks did with all their gods, you believe in an _____ God.
Theodore	**THE,** *god* The study of religion and the nature of divinity is known as _____ .

page 116

extraordinary 55	**EXTRA—,** *beyond, outside* When a country is permitted to maintain jurisdiction over its citizens in another country—citizens outside its own *territorial* limits—it enjoys _____ rights. 56
retrorockets 119	**RETRO—,** *backward, behind* The opposite of progression is _____. 120
statuesque 174	**—ESQUE,** *in the style of, like* Whatever suggests a charming *picture* is _____. 175
animal 239	**ANIM,** *feeling, disposition* A person who is lively and expressive in his looks and gestures is _____. 240
One that does not vary much, said especially of mild climates. 306	**EQUI, EQUA,** *equal* When a dispute—a lawsuit, let us say—is settled *equitably*, how is it settled? 307
He is devoted to enhancing his position, power, or wealth. 373	**HABIT,** *dwell, accustom* If you perform an act over and over, it soon becomes a _____ act. 374
comparable 440	**PAR,** *equal* What do we do when we *disparage* someone? 441

sensuous	**SENS, SENT**, *feel, think* The nerves which convey impressions to the brain and spinal cord are the _____ nerves.
507	508
It means "truly."	**VERB,** *word* A word which expresses action is a _____ .
572	573
epilepsy	**EPI—,** *on, upon, to* An inscription on a tomb is an _____ .
636	637
diphthong	**TRI,** *three* A pedaled vehicle with three wheels, especially one for children, is a _____ .
700	701
It spins them at high speeds.	**DEM,** *people* Whatever appeals to people of all sorts and conditions possesses a popular, or _____ , appeal.
761	762
anthropomorphic	**NEO,** *new* In 1898 two English chemists, William Ramsay and Morris Travers, discovered a new gas, now used in beacons and illuminated signs, and named it _____ .
826	827
theology	**THE,** *god* If a religion holds that God created the world and the people in it but thereafter did not interfere with them, it is called *deistic.* If it holds that God is still active in the world and in the lives of people, it is called _____ .
892	893

page 118

extraterritorial	**EXTRA—**, *beyond, outside* If you spend money beyond reasonable limits, you are _____ .
56	57
retrogression *or* regression	**RETRO—**, *backward, behind* An agreement, such as a wage settlement, which applies to a period of time before the agreement was reached is a _____ agreement.
120	121
picturesque	**—ESQUE**, *in the style of, like* Inspired by the buildings of the *Roman* Empire, a style of architecture which prevailed throughout Europe in the later Middle Ages is called _____ .
175	176
animated	**ANIM**, *feeling, disposition* Using the prefix IN—, finish this statement: An object that is apparently lifeless is _____ .
240	24!
It is settled fairly.	**EQUI, EQUA**, *equal* What kind of society is an *equalitarian* society?
307	308
habitual	**HABIT**, *dwell, accustom* A house that is fit to live in is _____ .
374	375
We belittle him.	**PAR**, *equal* When a jury notices a *disparity* in the statements of two witnesses, what does it notice?
441	442

page 119

sensory 508	**SENS, SENT,** *feel, think* Using the prefix EXTRA—, finish this sentence: Perception achieved through some means other than that of any of the ordinary senses is called _____ perception. 509
verb 573	**VERB,** *word* A short way of saying that a person has difficulty putting his thoughts into words is to say that he has difficulty in _____. 574
epitaph 637	**EPI—,** *on, upon, to* In the New Testament, the letters of advice and instruction which the Apostles sent to their correspondents are called the _____. 638
tricycle 701	**TRI,** *three* A series of three separate but related works—e.g., Theodore Dreiser's *The Financier, The Titan,* and *The Stoic*—is called a _____. 702
democratic 762	**DEM,** *people* Using the prefix EPI—, finish this statement: If a disease is widespread in a community, it is _____. 763
neon 827	**NEO,** *new* The root *phyte* means "plant." Any beginner, or any person newly initiated into anything—a new plant, as it were—is a _____. 828
theistic 893	**THE,** *god* Using the prefix A—, finish this statement: The belief that no God exists is called _____. 894

page 120

extravagant	**EXTRA—**, *beyond, outside* In school or college, sports and social events are referred to as _____ activities.
57	58
retroactive	**RETRO—**, *backward, behind* The root *spect* means "to look." If you look back and examine events after they have occurred, you examine them in _____ .
121	122
Romanesque	**—ESQUE,** *in the style of, like* This suffix is commonly attached to the names of writers, painters, and other notable people. A literary work in the style of *Kipling* is _____ ; a painting after the manner of *Raphael* is _____ ; a man who resembles Abraham *Lincoln* is _____ .
176	177
inanimate	**ANIM,** *feeling, disposition* Beginning with UN (a variant form of UNI), complete this sentence: When everyone in a group is of the same opinion, the group is _____ in its opinion.
241	242
One in which everyone has equal rights.	**ERR,** *err, wander* A conclusion that is not right is an _____ conclusion.
308	309
habitable	**HABIT,** *dwell, accustom* Another word for *house* or *dwelling* is _____ .
375	376
A disagrement or conflict between the two statements.	**PAR,** *equal* When is it appropriate to call an individual a *nonpareil*?
442	443

page 121

extrasensory

509

SENS, SENT, *feel, think*
Using the prefix PRE—, finish this statement: A feeling that something is going to happen is a _____.

510

verbalizing

574

VERB, *word*
If you quote someone word for word, you quote him _____.

575

Epistles

638

EPI—, *on, upon, to*
The root *gram* means "to write." A short, witty comment on some subject, whether written or spoken, is an _____.

639

trilogy

702

TRI, *three*
Besides *trio* and *trinity,* both of Latin origin, what is another word—this one of Greek origin—that designates a set of three?
_____

703

epidemic

763

DEM, *people*
Using the prefix EN—, finish this sentence: If a disease, although not widespread, is always present in an area—e.g., the common cold—it is _____.

764

neophyte

828

NEO, *new*
The root *lith* means "stone." The New Stone Age, characterized, among many other things, by the use of polished stone tools, is also called the _____ period.

829

atheism

894

THE, *god*
Using a word beginning with MONO, complete this statement: A belief in one God is known as _____.

page 122

895

extracurricular

INTER—, *between*
An agreement between two or more nations is an _____ agreement.

---

retrospect

Before proceeding to Frame 123, do Review 2 on page 139.

Kiplingesque,
Raphaelesque,
Lincolnesque

—IFEROUS, *bringing, producing*
Trees which produce *cones,* such as the pine and the cypress, are _____ trees.

---

unanimous

ANIM, *feeling, disposition*
The root *magn* means "great." A person who is noble and generous is a _____ person.

---

erroneous

ERR, *err, wander*
A medieval knight who wandered in search of adventures was known as a knight _____ .

---

habitation

HABIT, *dwell, accustom*
Using the prefix IN—, what is a word for one who lives in a house or dwelling? _____

When, in respect to some merit, he has no equal.

PART, *part, side*
A tiny piece or fragment of anything is a _____ .

page 123

presentiment

510

SENS, SENT, *feel, think*
When a group reaches a *consensus* in respect to some subject, what has it reached?

511

---

verbatim

575

VERB, *word*
What do we mean when we make the statement, which is always disparaging, that a person is *verbose*?

576

---

epigram

639

EPI—, *on, upon, to*
The root *thet* means "to put." If you heap abusive names or phrases on a person, you heap _____ on him.

640

---

triad

703

TRI, *three*
The root *pod* means "foot." A three-legged apparatus for supporting a camera is known as a _____ .

704

---

endemic

764

DEM, *people*
The root *agog(ue)* means "to lead." A politician who resorts to unscrupulous methods of stirring up the people in order to achieve personal power is a _____ .

765

---

neolithic

829

NEO, *new*
One of the meanings of the root *log* is "speech." When a new word or expression first appears, such as *flapper* in the twenties, *G.I.* in the forties, and *cosmonaut* in the sixties, it is known as a _____ .

830

---

monotheism

895

THE, *god*
Using a word beginning with POLY, complete this sentence: A belief in many gods is known as _____ .

page 124

896

international

INTER—, *between*
A contest between two colleges is an _____ contest.

59   60

SE—, *away from*
In 1860 and 1861, eleven Southern states _____ from the Union.

123

---

coniferous

—IFEROUS, *bringing, producing*
Whatever produces an *odor* is _____ .

178   179

---

magnanimous

ANIM, *feeling, disposition*
This root does not necessarily mean *good* feeling or disposition. When a person is hostile, he is expressing _____ .

243   244

---

errant

ERR, *err, wander*
Using the prefix AB—, complete this statement: If an individual's mind strays from reasonable channels, he is experiencing mental _____ .

310   311

---

inhabitant

HABIT, *dwell, accustom*
Using the prefix CO—, complete this sentence: When a man and woman live together as husband and wife, they are said to _____ .

377   378

---

particle

PART, *part, side*
If you divide something—a room, let us say—into separate parts, you _____ it.

444   page 125   445

It has reached an agreement of opinion.

511

SENS, SENT, *feel, think*
Why is man called a *sentient* being?

512

We mean he uses more words than are necessary.

576

VERB, *word*
When we refer to an individual's utterances as just so much *verbiage*, what do we mean?

577

---

epithets

640

EPI—, *on, upon, to*
One of the meanings of the root *log(ue)* is "speech." A section attached as a final commentary to the end of a literary work—such as a novel or a play—is an _____ .

641

---

tripod

704

TRI, *three*
The root *ptych* means "fold" or "panel." A picture or carving in three panels, often used as an altarpiece, is called a _____ .

705

---

demagogue *or* demagog

765

DEM, *people*
One of the meanings of the root *graphy* is "science." The science which collects and studies the vital statistics of a population—births, deaths, marriages, etc.—is known as _____ .

766

---

neologism

830

NEO, *new*
The esthetic standards of *classical* Greece and Rome enjoyed such a vogue in the arts and manners of late seventeenth- and early eighteenth-century England that scholars often call this age in English history the _____ period.

831

---

polytheism

896

THE, *god*
Beginning with PAN, finish this sentence: If a people believe in more than one god, as did the Greeks and Romans, all their gods together constitute their _____ .

897

intercollegiate	**INTER—,** *between* The period of time between two acts in a play is called an _____ .
seceded	**SE—,** *away from* A person who conceals his thoughts and plans is a _____ person.
odoriferous	**—IFEROUS,** *bringing, producing* Anything that carries infection or disease—certain *pests*, for instance—is _____ .
animosity	**AQUA, AQUE,** *water* A single board pulled by a motorboat and ridden by a person standing up is called an _____ .
aberrations	**ERR,** *err, wander* What do we mean when we declare that an individual is *erratic*?
cohabit	**HABIT,** *dwell, accustom* What place are we speaking of when we speak of an animal's natural *habitat*?
partition	**PART,** *part, side* A person who definitely favors and supports a particular cause is a _____ of that cause.

Because he feels, perceives, and thinks. 512	**SIMIL, SIMUL,** *like, similar* A figure of speech in which two different things are likened to one another—"My love is like a red red rose"—is known as a _____. 513
We mean his utterances are wordy but do not say much. 577	**VERT, VERS,** *turn* The bones which make up a person's spinal column and enable him to turn in various ways are known as _____. 578
epilogue 641	**EU—,** *good* One of the meanings of the root *gen* is "race." A popular first name for men which means well-born is _____. 642
triptych 705	NOTE: Greek and Latin are sister languages, both of them offshoots of the earlier Indo-European language. Furthermore, they borrowed many words from one another. Consequently, many Greek and Latin elements are similar or identical in form and meaning, such as the
demography 766	**DYNA,** *power* Alfred Nobel, the Swedish industrialist who endowed the Nobel Prizes, invented an explosive in 1866 which he named _____. 767
neoclassical *or* neoclassic 831	**ONYM,** *name, meaning, pronunciation* Using the prefix AN—, complete this sentence: If a book is published without the name of the author, it is published _____. 832
pantheon 897	**THE—,** *god* The root *crat* means "rule." When a priestly class, ruling in the name of God, governs a country, as was partially the case in Puritan New England, the system of government is called a _____ system. 898

page 128

intermission	**INTER—**, *between* The root *stell* means "star." What, then, is *interstellar* space?	
61		62
secretive	**SE—**, *away from* The root *clus* means "to shut." If an individual has shut himself away from others, he has gone into _____.	
124		125
pestiferous	**—IFEROUS**, *bringing, producing* The root *voc* means "voice." The word that describes a person who speaks in a loud and clamorous voice is _____.	
180		181
aquaplane	**AQUA, AQUE**, *water* A tank or pool for water animals and water plants is an _____.	
245		246
We mean his conduct is unsteady and irregular.	**FAC, FACT**, *make, do* An industrial building in which articles of one kind or another are made is a _____.	
312		313
We are speaking of the place where it normally lives.	**HABIT**, *dwell, accustom* What do we mean when we refer to an individual as a *habitué* of some place—e.g., a club or café?	
379		380
partisan	**PART**, *part, side* Using the prefix IM—, what is a word that describes a person who, in judging a dispute or contest, is fair and unbiased? _____	
446	*page 129*	447

simile 513	**SIMIL, SIMUL,** *like, similar* If you assume an attitude that you do not actually feel, you _____ the attitude. 514
vertebrae *or* vertebras 578	**VERT, VERS,** *turn* In medicine, the symptom of dizziness is called _____. 579
Eugene 642	**EU—,** *good* The science which investigates hereditary factors in order to improve races and breeds is called _____. 643
	Greek DI and TRI on the one hand and the Latin DU and TRI on the other. But most Greek elements combine only with Greek elements, most Latin elements only with Latin elements.
dynamite 767	**DYNA,** *power* A forceful and energetic person is commonly spoken of as a _____ person. 768
anonymously 832	**ONYM,** *name, meaning, pronunciation* Using the prefix SYN—, finish this sentence: Words of the same or similar meaning—e.g., *ardent* and *passionate*—are called _____. 833
theocratic 898	Now turn to Review 3 on page 165.

The space between stars. 62	**INTER—,** *between* The root *regn* means "to rule." What is an *interregnum*? 63
seclusion 125	**SE—,** *away from* The root *duc* means "to lead." If you have been led away from your duty—especially in an artful or persuasive way—you have been _____ from it. 126
vociferous 181	# 4 Latin Numbers (Frames 182–221)
aquarium 246	**AQUA, AQUE,** *water* A shade of bluish-green which approximates the color of marine water is called _____. 247
factory 313	**FAC, FACT,** *make, do* If a person performs a task easily, he performs it with _____. 314
We mean he is a person who frequently visits the place. 380	**LINE,** *line* A man who sets up and repairs telephone lines is known as a _____. 381
impartial 447	**PART,** *part, side* Using the prefix NON—, finish this sentence: An election in which candidates run without party designation, as in many cities, is a _____ election. 448

page 131

simulate

514

SIMIL, SIMUL, *like, similar*
Using the prefix DIS–, complete this sentence: An individual who conceals his feelings—often in order to gain some advantage—is said to _____.

515

vertigo

579

VERT, VERS, *turn*
Using the prefix AD–, complete this sentence: A person who has turned toward you in hostility is your _____.

580

eugenics

643

EU–, *good*
One of the meanings of the root *logy* is "speech." A speech in high praise of someone or something is a _____.

644

TETRA, *four*
A liquid, used in cleaning fluids and in fire extinguishers, which is made up of one part carbon for every four parts of chlorine is called carbon _____.

706

dynamic

768

DYNA, *power*
A machine for producing electrical energy is called a _____.

769

synonyms

833

ONYM, *name, meaning, pronunciation*
Using the prefix ANT–, finish this statement: Words of opposite meaning—e.g., *love* and *hate*—are called _____.

834

page 132

The period between two rulers, when a country or group is without its usual head. 63	**INTER—**, *between* What kind of pain is *intermittent* pain? 64
seduced 126	**SEMI—**, *half, partly* A half circle is also called a _____. 127
	UNI, *one* One of the purposes of the American Constitution, as stated in its Preamble, is "to form a more perfect _____." 182
aquamarine 247	**AQUA, AQUE**, *water* The root *duct* means "to lead." A conduit for bringing water from a distance is an _____. 248
facility 314	**FAC, FACT**, *make, do* The root *bene* means "good." An individual who does many good things for you is your _____. 315
lineman 381	**LINE**, *line* An individual's line of ancestors constitutes his _____. 382
nonpartisan 448	**PART**, *part, side* Using the prefix BI—, complete this statement: A proposal in Congress supported by both parties enjoys _____ support. 449

page 133

dissimulate

SIMIL, SIMUL, *like, similar*
When one group of people *assimilates* another group, what is the result?

Continued on page 2.

---

adversary

VERT, VERS, *turn*
Using the prefix IN—, complete this statement: Animals that do not possess spinal columns are known as _____.

---

eulogy

EU—, *good*
The root *phon* means "sound." What kind of voice is a *euphonious* voice?

---

tetrachloride

TETRA, *four*
The root *meter* means "measure." If most of the lines of a poem contain four measures—Poe's "To Helen" is an example—we say the poem is written in _____.

---

dynamo

DYNA, *power*
A ruling family, such as the Tudors in England, the Bourbons in France and Spain, or the Romanovs in Russia, is called a _____.

---

antonyms

ONYM, *name, meaning, pronunciation*
The root *hom* means "same." Words which are the same in pronunciation but different in meaning, and often in origin and spelling—e.g., *tea* and *tee*—are _____.

Pain that comes from time to time —i.e., between periods without pain 64	Before proceeding to Frame 65, turn to Review 1 on page 137.
semicircle 127	**SEMI—**, *half, partly* Workers who are only partly skilled are _____ . Continued on page 1. 128
Union 182	**UNI**, *one* A soldier's dress, because it is the same as that of his fellows, is called a _____ . 183
aqueduct 248	**AQUA, AQUE**, *water* What kind of plants are *aquatic* plants? 249
benefactor 315	**FAC, FACT**, *make, do* The root *male* means "evil." A person who does evil things is a _____ . 316
lineage 382	**LINE**, *line* Using the prefix DE—, what is a word that means *sketch* or *depict*? _____ . 383
bipartisan 449	**PART**, *part, side* What is a *tripartite* agreement? Continued at the top of page 2. 450

Latin Prefixes: Review 1

I Give the English meanings for each of these Latin prefixes. The answers for this and the following exercises will be found on the back of this page.

1. AB—, ABS— _____
2. ANTE— _____
3. BI— _____
4. CIRCUM— _____
5. COUNTER—, CONTRA— _____

II Give the Latin prefix for each of these English meanings.

1. off, down, the reverse _____
2. half, less than usual _____
3. opposite of, away from _____
4. out _____
5. beyond, outside _____
6. between _____

III The list of words at the right contains one word in illustration of each of the Latin prefixes we have studied so far—a word which you have already encountered in the exercises that preceded this review. Select the word that will appropriately complete each of the following sentences.

1. After due deliberation, the jury decided to _____ the defendant.

2. At one time America and several other countries enjoyed _____ rights in China.

3. He was proud of the fact that one of his _____ had fought in the American Revolution.

4. For months after her mother's death, she was _____.

5. He did not get along well with his father, who always _____ his activities.

6. The dentist told him his last remaining _____ would have to be extracted.

7. Under pressure from his colleagues, he _____ the opinions he had formerly expressed.

8. He remained so excited that he suffered from an _____ fever.

9. Despite their maneuvers, they were not able to _____ the new regulations.

10. His athletic prowess was so great that some of his fellow-students regarded him as a _____.

11. He changed his mind and decided to _____ his previous order.

abjure
antecedents
bicuspid
circumvent
countermand
demigod
depreciated
disconsolate
exonerate
extraterritorial
intermittent

page 137

ANSWERS

I 1. from, away; 2. before; 3. two, twice; 4. around; 5. opposite, against.

II 1. de—; 2. demi—; 3. dis—; 4. ex—, e—; 5. extra—; 6. inter—.

III 1. exonerate; 2. extraterritorial; 3. antecedents; 4. disconsolate; 5. deprecated; 6. bicuspid; 7. abjured; 8. intermittent; 9. circumvent; 10. demigod; 11. counterma[nd]

Resume Latin prefixes on page 1, frame 65.

Latin Prefixes: Review 2

I Give the English meanings for each of these Latin prefixes. The answers for this and the following exercises will be found on the back of this page.

1. INTRA–, INTRO– _____
2. MIS– _____
3. NON– _____
4. PER– _____
5. RETRO– _____

II Give the Latin prefix for each of these English meanings.

1. after _____
2. before _____
3. forth; in front of; instead of _____
4. largely, almost, seemingly _____
5. again, back _____

III The list of words at the right contains one word in illustration of each of the last ten Latin prefixes. Select the word that will complete each of the following sentences.

1. As president of the company, he was more successful than his _____ had been.
2. His acquaintances paid no attention to him. They regarded him as a _____.
3. When we consider our childhood in _____ _____ it often seems happier than it actually was.
4. The Federal Communications Commission, which supervises radio and television activities, is a _____ agency.
5. Defeats did not discourage him for long because he had a _____ temperament.
6. When we call a grown man a boy we are using a _____.
7. She visited the clinic in order to receive training in the _____ care of her baby.
8. He understood his own motives because he was _____.
9. His judgments were accurate so often that he soon won a reputation for being a _____ individual.
10. Robert Browning's many works make him one of the most _____ poets in the English-speaking world.

introspective
misnomer
nonentity
perspicacious
postnatal
predecessor
prolific
quasi-judicial
resilient
retrospect

page 139

ANSWERS

I   1. into, within; 2. wrong; 3. not, without; 4. through or throughout, by; 5. backward, behind.

II   1. after; 2. pre—; 3. pro—; 4. quasi—; 5. re—.

III   1. predecessor; 2. nonentity; 3. retrospect; 4. quasi-judicial; 5. resilient; 6. misnomer; 7. postnatal; 8. introspective; 9. perspicacious; 10. prolific.

Resume Latin prefixes on page 125, frame 123.

Latin Prefixes: Review 3

I Give the English meaning for each of these Latin prefixes. The answers for this and the following exercises will be found on the back of this page.

1. SE— _____
2. SEMI— _____
3. SUPER— _____
4. TRANS— _____

II Give the Latin prefix for each of these English meanings.

1. exceedingly, beyond _____
2. to, toward _____
3. with, together _____
4. not _____
5. under, less _____

III Select from the list at the right the word that will complete each of the following sentences.

1. When called upon to speak, he suddenly became _____.
2. After he went bankrupt, even his enemies _____ with him.
3. The police reported that the suspect lived in virtual _____.
4. He was so patriotic that some people criticized him for being _____.
5. He alienated many people because of his _____ manner.
6. People in the audience began to leave because the speaker made the same point _____.
7. Because his temperament was naturally cheerful, his feelings of dejection were only _____.
8. His personality was so commanding that all his associates were _____ to him.
9. The reunion was so successful that the family decided to make it a _____ affair.

ad nauseam
commiserated
inarticulate
seclusion
semiannual
subservient
supercilious
transitory
ultranationalistic

ANSWERS

I 1. away from; 2. half, partly; 3. above, beyond; 4. across, through, beyond.

II 1. ultra—; 2. ad—; 3. com—; 4. in—; 5. sub—.

III 1. inarticulate; 2. commiserated; 3. seclusion; 4. ultranationalistic; 5. supercilious; 6. ad nauseam; 7. transitory; 8. subservient; 9. semiannual.

Begin Latin suffixes and numbers on page 101.

Latin Numbers: Review

I Give the English meaning for each of these Latin elements. The answers for this and the following exercises will be found on the back of this page.

1. **UNI** _____
2. **DU** _____
3. **TRI** _____
4. **QUADR** _____
5. **QUINT** _____
6. **SEX** _____

II Give the Latin element for each of these English meanings.

1. seven _____
2. eight _____
3. nine _____
4. ten _____
5. hundred _____
6. thousand _____

III Select from the list at the right the word that will complete each of the following sentences.

1. In the year 1001, the Christian era entered its second _____.
2. All protozoans are _____ animals.
3. As a devout Roman Catholic, she performed a _____ at regular intervals.
4. The U. S. Bureau of the Census counts the population in America every _____.
5. Having been caught in a series of misrepresentations, he became known for his _____.
6. Many jazz bands consist of a _____ of musicians.
7. An individual in his sixties is a _____.
8. In 1876 many _____ celebrations occurred in honor of the American Declaration of Independence.
9. One of the problems we encounter in geometry is how to _____ an angle.
10. The first eight lines of a sonnet are sometimes called the _____.
11. A person in his seventies is a _____.
12. Man has learned how to make use of the horse, the cow, and many another _____.

centennial
decade
duplicity
millennium
novena
octet
quadruped
quintet
septuagenarian
sexagenarian
trisect
unicellular

page 143

ANSWERS

I 1. one; 2. two; 3. three; 4. four; 5. five; 6. six.

II 1. sept; 2. oct; 3. nov; 4. dec; 5. cent; 6. mill.

III 1. millennium; 2. unicellular; 3. novena; 4. decade; 5. duplicity; 6. quintet; 7. sexagenarian; 8. centennial; 9. trisect; 10. octet; 11. septuagenarian; 12. quadruped.

Begin Latin roots on page 79.

Latin Roots: Review 1

I Give the English meaning for each of these Latin roots. The answers for this and the following exercises will be found on the back of this page.

1. ALI _____
2. ALTER _____
3. AM _____
4. ANIM _____
5. AQUA, AQUE _____

II Give the Latin root for each of these English meanings.

1. weapon, arm _____
2. flesh _____
3. body _____
4. believe, trust _____
5. run, go _____

III Select from the list at the right the word that will complete each of the following sentences.

1. He prided himself on the fact that he had always lived in _____ with his neighbors.

2. Poets and philosophers often lament the _____ woes of man.

3. He protested that his _____ rights were being curtailed.

4. Following the _____, the two countries resumed peaceful relations.

5. Having always lived near the ocean, he was especially interested in _____ life.

6. For years he had been in such friendly association with his partner that he regarded him as his _____.

7. The lawyer, being negligent, gave the documents only a _____ inspection.

8. They had quarreled so often that they felt nothing but _____ towards one another.

9. After the _____ of the battle, the shattered enemy forces retreated.

10. He was an easy mark for unscrupulous salesmen, for he was a _____ person.

alter ego
amity
animosity
aquatic
armistice
carnage
corporeal
credulous
cursory
inalienable

ANSWERS

I 1. other, another; 2. other, another; 3. love, friend; 4. feeling, disposition; 5. water.

II 1. arm; 2. carn; 3. corp; 4. cred; 5. curr, cur.

III 1. amity; 2. corporeal; 3. inalienable; 4. armistice; 5. aquatic; 6. alter ego; 7. cursory; 8. animosity; 9. carnage; 10. credulous.

Resume Latin roots on page 87, frame 292.

Latin Roots: Review 2

I Give the English meaning for each of these Latin roots. The answers for this and the following exercises will be found on the back of this page.

1. DIC _____
2. EQUI, EQUA _____
3. ERR _____
4. FAC, FACT _____
5. FID _____

II Give the Latin root for each of these English meanings.

1. form, shape _____
2. bend, turn _____
3. flow _____
4. form, rule _____
5. go, step _____

III Select from the list at the right the word that will complete each of the following sentences.

1. Many people who seem unfriendly are merely _____.

2. Before deciding where to dig, the prospector studied the _____ of the hills.

3. Despite the vexing nature of the task, he retained his _____.

4. In her anger, she hurled a _____ at him.

5. Instead of sticking to the point, he rambled on in an endless _____.

6. Unlike his thoughtless brother, he was a _____ person.

7. Cairo, Illinois, is situated at the _____ of the Ohio and Mississippi Rivers.

8. He liked the statue so well that he commissioned a sculptor to make a _____ of it.

9. Ever since he received a blow on the head, people have noticed _____ in his conduct.

10. Besides being good reading, the book possessed an attractive _____.

aberrations
configuration
confluence
diffident
digression
equanimity
facsimile
format
malediction
reflective

page 147

ANSWERS

I   1. say; 2. equal; 3. err, wander; 4. make, do; 5. faith.

II   1. figur; 2. flex, flect; 3. flu; 4. form; 5. grad, gress.

III   1. diffident; 2. configuration; 3. equanimity; 4. malediction; 5. digression; 6. reflective; 7. confluence; 8. facsimile; 9. aberrations; 10. format.

Resume Latin roots on page 97, frame 364.

Latin Roots: Review 3

I Give the English meaning for each of these Latin roots. The answers for this and the following exercises will be found on the back of this page.

1. GRAN _____
2. GRAND _____
3. HABIT _____
4. LINE _____
5. LOC _____

II Give the Latin root for each of these English meanings.

1. speak _____
2. great, large _____
3. bad _____
4. mother _____
5. middle _____

III Select from the list at the right the word that will complete each of the following sentences.

1. The artist set himself to _____ the model's features.
2. A zoo is not an elephant's natural _____.
3. The city discovered that it had not _____ enough resources for slum clearance.
4. Concerned only with his own welfare, he did nothing that did not contribute to his _____.
5. He preferred powdered sugar to _____ sugar.
6. Many people regard Beethoven's Fifth Symphony as his _____.
7. Whenever his relatives got into a fight, he acted as an _____.
8. He said that his mother was so dominating that he had grown up in a _____ family.
9. Despite his fatigue and lack of appetite, he insisted that he was experiencing only a _____.
10. The negotiators retired to the conference room where they could carry on their _____.

allocated

colloquy

delineate

granulated

habitat

intermediary

magnum opus

malaise

matriarchal

self-aggrandizement

page 149

ANSWERS

I   1. grain, seed; 2. great; 3. dwell, accustom; 4. line; 5. place.

II   1. loq, locut; 2. magn; 3. mal; 4. mater, matr; 5. med.

III   1. delineate; 2. habitat; 3. allocated; 4. self-aggrandizement; 5. granulated; 6. magnum opus; 7. intermediary; 8. matriarchal; 9. malaise; 10. colloquy.

Resume Latin roots on page 87, frame 426.

Latin Roots: Review 4

I Give the English meaning for each of these Latin roots. The answers for this and the following exercises will be found on the back of this page.

1. MEMOR _____
2. ORDIN, ORDAIN _____
3. PAR _____
4. PART _____
5. PASS _____

II Give the Latin root for each of these English meanings.

1. father, fatherland _____
2. hang _____
3. person _____
4. to please or appease _____
5. place, put _____

III Select from the list at the right the word that will complete each of the following sentences.

1. There was always a great _____ between his promises and his performance.

2. Having grown tired of life in America, he decided to become an _____.

3. Despite all accusations, his countenance remained _____.

4. After much practice, he became skillful at _____ _____ writing.

5. In disputes between his mother and father, he was usually his father's _____.

6. She looked back on her honeymoon as the most _____ time of her life.

7. His jowls were _____, like those of a bulldog.

8. His constant demands for money were so _____ _____ that his family finally threw him out.

9. The judge had acquired a reputation for being the very _____ of honesty.

10. Many attempts were made to diminish his enmity, but he remained _____.

disparity
expatriate
expository
impassive
implacable
inordinate
memorable
partisan
pendulous
personification

ANSWERS

I   1. memory; 2. order; 3. equal; 4. part, side; 5. feel.

II   1. pater, patr; 2. pend; 3. person; 4. plac; 5. pos, pon.

III   1. disparity; 2. expatriate; 3. impassive; 4. expository; 5. partisan; 6. memorable; 7. pendulous; 8. inordinate; 9. personification; 10. implacable.

Resume Latin roots on page 78, frame 488.

Latin Roots: Review 5

I Give the English meaning for each of these Latin roots. The answers for this and the following exercises will be found on the back of this page.

1. POTENT _____
2. PRIM _____
3. RUPT _____
4. SENS, SENT _____
5. SIMIL, SIMUL _____

II Give the Latin root for each of these English meanings.

1. sound _____
2. look _____
3. time _____
4. hold _____
5. earth, land _____

III Select from the list at the right the word that will complete each of the following sentences.

1. No one was taken in by his _____ arguments.

2. Man has always bewailed the woes of his _____ existence.

3. His true feelings were apparent in spite of his efforts to _____.

4. He had made such a success of everything he had attempted that at times he felt _____.

5. His voice was not _____ enough for a concert singer.

6. The commanding officer decided that the position of his troops was not _____.

7. When asked a direct question, he would _____.

8. The company was disturbed by the _____ departure of several guests.

9. He could not rid himself of a _____ that an accident would occur.

10. The wilderness, untouched by man, remained in its _____ state.

abrupt
dissimulate
omnipotent
presentiment
primeval
resonant
specious
temporize
tenable
terrestrial

page 153

ANSWERS

I   1. power; 2. first; 3. break; 4. feel, think; 5. like, similar.

II   1. son; 2. spec, spect; 3. temp, tempor; 4. ten; 5. terr, terra, ter.

III   1. specious; 2. terrestrial; 3. dissimulate; 4. omnipotent; 5. resonant; 6. tenable; 7. temporize; 8. abrupt; 9. presentiment; 10. primeval.

Resume Latin roots on page 74, frame 551.

Latin Roots: Review 6

I Give the English meaning for each of these Latin roots. The answers for this and the following exercises will be found on the back of this page.

1. TRACT _____
2. TRIBUT _____
3. VAG _____
4. VEN _____
5. VER _____

II Give the Latin root for each of these English meanings.

1. word _____
2. turn _____
3. see _____
4. life (2) _____
5. call _____

III Select from the list at the right the word that will complete each of the following sentences.

1. He decided to loaf during the _____ _____ time.

2. Unlike his brother, who always used the fewest words possible, his conversation was _____ _____.

3. He would not now be living on the charity of his relatives if he had not been _____ all his life.

4. He was considered odd because of the _____ _____ that characterized his conduct.

5. He always enjoyed attending parties, for he was naturally _____.

6. Whenever the subject of war came up, he would always _____ to his own experiences as a soldier.

7. The house was so hot and humid that it was a _____ steam bath.

8. It was hard to know what he meant, for his statements were _____.

9. Despite all efforts to manage him, his parents found him _____.

10. Countries usually do not go to war unless they think their _____ interests are endangered.

11. His conscience finally drove him to make _____ for the injustice he had done.

advert
convivial
equivocal
improvident
intervening
intractable
retribution
vagaries
verbose
veritable
vital

page 155

ANSWERS

I   1. draw, pull; 2. give; 3. wander; 4. come, go; 5. true.

II   1. verb; 2. vert, vers; 3. vis, vid: 4. vit, viv; 5. voc, vok.

III   1. intervening; 2. verbose; 3. improvident; 4. vagaries; 5. convivial; 6. advert; 7. veritable; 8. equivocal; 9. intractable; 10. vital; 11. retribution.

Turn now to page 58 for Greek prefixes.

Greek Prefixes: Review

I Give the English meaning for each of these Greek prefixes. The answers for this and the following exercises will be found on the back of this page.

1. A–, AN– _____
2. ANTI–, ANT– _____
3. APO– _____
4. CATA– _____
5. DIA– _____
6. EPI– _____

II Give the Greek prefix for each of these English meanings.

1. good _____
2. out, outside _____
3. excessive _____
4. under, deficient _____
5. alongside of, with _____
6. about, around, near _____
7. together, with _____

III Select from the list at the right the word that will complete each of the following sentences.

1. After leaving the organization, he was denounced by those who remained as an _____.

2. When the patient described his symptoms, the doctor immediately recognized the _____ _____.

3. He was generally looked upon as an _____ _____ because of his unique habits.

4. The dancers wore filmy dresses that were almost _____.

5. Being a witty person, he was fond of answering a question with an _____.

6. It had been a violent year, filled with both natural and man-made _____.

7. He declared that, in view of what they had done to him, he would always be their _____.

8. Her speech seemed affected because it was full of _____.

9. After examining him, the doctor announced that his liver was _____.

10. Before coming to the main point, they discussed _____ matters.

11. His friends tried to change his mind, but he remained _____.

12. The expression "She weighs a ton" is a _____ _____.

13. It took them several hours to pack all their _____ for the camping trip.

adamant
antagonist
apostate
cataclysms
diaphanous
eccentric
epigram
euphemisms
hyperbole
hypoactive
paraphernalia
peripheral
syndrome

page 157

ANSWERS

I   1. not, without; 2. against; 3. away from; 4. down; 5. across, through; 6. on, upon, to.

II   1. eu—; 2. exo—, ec—, ex—; 3. hyper—; 4. hypo—; 5. para—; 6. peri—; 7. syn—, sym—.

III   1. apostate; 2. syndrome; 3. eccentric; 4. diaphanous; 5. epigram; 6. cataclysms; 7. antagonist; 8. euphemisms; 9. hypoactive; 10. peripheral; 11. adamant; 12. hyperbole; 13. paraphernalia.

For Greek suffixes and numbers, turn to page 74.

Greek Numbers: Review

I Give the English meaning for each of these Greek prefixes. The answers for this and the following exercises will be found on the back of this page.

1. MONO— _____
2. DI _____
3. TRI _____
4. TETRA _____
5. PENTA _____
6. HEXA _____

II Give the Greek element for each of these English meanings.

1. seven _____
2. eight _____
3. nine _____
4. ten _____
5. hundred _____
6. thousand _____

III Select from the list at the right the word that will complete each of the following sentences.

1. The second book of the Old Testament relates how Moses received the _____ from God.
2. At one time England was divided into seven kingdoms which historians refer to as the _____.
3. The word *toy* contains a _____.
4. Anything with eight sides or angles can be called an _____.
5. Instead of saying a hundred grams, a scientist may say a _____.
6. In Europe, the _____ is used to measure distance instead of the mile.
7. When each line of a poem generally contains four metrical feet, we say it is written in _____.
8. As a Biblical scholar he specialized in the study of the _____.
9. Shakespeare's *King Henry VI*, written in three self-contained parts, constitutes a _____.
10. An animal with six feet is called a _____.
11. He kept harping on the same subject so often that people asserted that he suffered from a _____.
12. A single word for nine people or things is _____.

Decalogue
diphthong
ennead
hectogram
Heptarchy
hexapod
kilometer
monomania
octagon
Pentateuch
tetrameter
trilogy

page 159

ANSWERS

I 1. one; 2. two; 3. three; 4. four; 5. five; 6. six.

II 1. hepta; 2. oct; 3. ennea; 4. dec; 5. hecto; 6. kilo.

III 1. Decalogue; 2. Heptarchy; 3. diphthong; 4. octagon; 5. hectogram; 6. kilometer; 7. tetrameter; 8. Pentateuch; 9. trilogy; 10. hexapod; 11. monomania; 12. ennead.

For Greek roots, turn now to page 44.

Greek Roots: Review 1

I Give the English meaning for each of these Greek roots. The answers for this and the following exercises will be found on the back of this page.

1. ANTHROP _____
2. ARCH _____
3. AUTO _____
4. BIO _____
5. CHRON _____

II Give the Greek root for each of these English meanings.

1. circle _____
2. people _____
3. power _____
4. marriage _____
5. earth _____

III Select from the list at the right the word that will complete each of the following sentences.

1. He exercised such arbitrary and willful power over his family that his wife and children regarded him as an _____.

2. He avoided people so constantly that he became known as a _____.

3. The physician soon cured the disease by using _____.

4. The priest read with great care the latest _____ _____ of the Pope.

5. After several unsuccessful marriages, he became a _____.

6. Being interested in both statistics and people he decided to specialize in _____.

7. After much hesitation, they decided to build their house in the _____ style.

8. Not content to be simply a pilot, he set out to master the science of _____.

9. As far as modern warfare is concerned, the sword is an _____.

10. It was common knowledge that a few influential individuals constituted the organization's _____.

aerodynamics
anachronism
antibiotics
autocrat
demography
encyclical
Georgian
misanthrope
misogamist
oligarchy

page 161

ANSWERS

I 1. man; 2. first, chief; 3. self; 4. life; 5. time.

II 1. cycl; 2. dem; 3. dyna; 4. gam; 5. geo.

III 1. autocrat; 2. misanthrope; 3. antibiotics; 4. encyclical; 5. misogamist; 6. demography; 7. Georgian; 8. aerodynamics; 9. anachronism; 10. oligarchy.

Resume Greek roots on page 32, frame 785.

Greek Roots: Review 2

I Give the English meaning for each of these Greek roots. The answers for this and the following exercises will be found on the back of this page.

1. GRAPH, GRAM _____
2. HYDR _____
3. LEON, LION _____
4. LOG(UE), LOGY _____
5. MEGA, MEGALO _____

II Give the Greek root for each of these English meanings.

1. small _____
2. form _____
3. new _____
4. name, meaning, pronunciation _____
5. eye, view _____

III Select from the list at the right the word that will complete each of the following sentences.

1. Because he disliked publicity, he decided to make his large donation _____.
2. Although he had been with the company for over a year, he was still regarded by the older employees as a _____.
3. The teacher asked his students to produce a _____ of the book they had read.
4. He was so full of grandiose projects that people said he was afflicted with _____.
5. After the success of his play, he was _____ everywhere he went.
6. The library possessed many rare volumes that had been reproduced on _____.
7. After studying ultraviolet rays, he wrote a _____ on the subject.
8. Any conversation with him soon became a _____ on his part.
9. If a person works for many hours under a hot sun, he may become _____.
10. After he got married, his friends declared that his character had undergone a _____.

anonymously
dehydrated
lionized
megalomania
metamorphosis
microfilm
monograph
monologue
neophyte
synopsis

page 163

ANSWERS

I 1. writing, description; 2. water; 3. lion; 4. speech, study, collection; 5. large, great.

II 1. micro; 2. morph; 3. neo; 4. onym; 5. opt, ops.

III 1. anonymously; 2. neophyte; 3. synopsis; 4. megalomania; 5. lionized; 6. microfilm; 7. monograph; 8. monologue; 9. dehydrated; 10. metamorphosis.

Resume Greek roots on page 22, frame 845.

Greek Roots: Review 3

I Give the English meaning for each of these Greek roots. The answers for this and the following exercises will be found on the back of this page.

1. PAN _____
2. PATH _____
3. PHIL, PHILE _____
4. POLIT, POLIS _____

II Give the Greek root for each of these English meanings.

1. many _____
2. first, fundamental _____
3. see _____
4. god _____

III Select from the list at the right the word that will complete each of the following sentences.

1. His long study of English history had made an _____ of him.

2. Hamlet is the _____ of Shakespeare's most famous play.

3. As the result of long residence in many countries, he regarded himself as a _____.

4. Christians, Jews, and Moslems believe in _____.

5. One of the instruments a heart specialist uses most often is the _____.

6. The announcement created _____ among the crowd.

7. Despite the speaker's best efforts, the audience remained _____.

8. Because the company did business in several countries, it required a number of employees who were _____.

Anglophile
apathetic
cosmopolite
monotheism
pandemonium
polylingual
protagonist
stethoscope

ANSWERS

I   1. all; 2. feeling, disease; 3. love; 4. civic, city, citizen.

II   1. poly; 2. proto; 3. scop; 4. the.

III   1. Anglophile; 2. protagonist; 3. cosmopolite; 4. monotheism; 5. stethoscope; 6. pandemonium; 7. apathetic; 8. polylingual.

Words from the Names of People

The names of various people have entered into the language and become words. During the reign of Louis XIV, for instance, a French officer named Martinet acquired such a reputation as a drillmaster that *martinet* is now a word for any severe disciplinarian. To cite another example, the proud, cynical and romantic personality of Byron, the English poet, impressed the world so vividly that *Byronic* has become a word which describes this kind of personality. And sometimes a person's name has become a word simply because something was named after him. Thus, a certain unit of electrical power received the designation *watt* in tribute to James Watt, the Scottish inventor of the steam engine.

As these examples illustrate, words which are derived from the names of people are capitalized in some cases. Furthermore, they may have acquired a grammatical ending, as in *Byronic*, or, as in *martinet* and *watt*, they may not.

In these exercises, an individual's name is italicized and followed by a brief statement identifying him. On the line below, write the word derived from the name and a short definition of the word, as has been done with the first example. Use the dictionary freely.

Bégon, A French administrator and patron of science.

begonia—an ornamental plant.   899

Bloomer, an American woman who became famous as a social reformer in the nineteenth century.
      900

Bowdler, an Englishman who edited Shakespeare's works.
      901

Boycott, a land agent in Ireland who was ostracized by his neighbors for refusing to reduce rents.
      902

Boysen, an American botanist who developed a certain berry.
      903

Burnside, a bewhiskered Union general in the American Civil War.
      904

Cardigan, an English earl for whom an article of clothing was named.
      905

Chauvin, A French soldier noted for his extravagant devotion to Napoleon.
      906

Comstock, an American reformer with a particular zeal for protecting public morals.
      907

Dahl, a Swedish botanist of the eighteenth century.
      908

Derrick, a London hangman of the seventeenth century.
      909

Doily, a London dealer in cloth during the seventeenth century.
      910

Draco, an Athenian statesman who drew up an especially severe code of laws.

911

Galvani, an Italian physicist who experimented in electricity.

912

Garden, a botanist born in Scotland who emigrated to America.

913

Guillotin, a Frenchman who, during the French Revolution, advocated a certain form of capital punishment.

914

Jeremiah, an Old Testament prophet with a fiery tongue.

915

Jezebel, a wicked queen in the Old Testament.

916

John Hancock, a signer of the American Declaration of Independence.

917

MacAdam, a Scottish engineer who devised a method of building roads.

918

Machiavelli, a Florentine political philosopher of the Renaissance who wrote *The Prince.*

919

MacIntosh, a Scotchman who invented a new fabric.

920

Mae West, a famous American actress.

921

Magnol, a French physician and botanist.

922

Maverick, a Texas rancher who, unlike his neighbors, did not brand his calves.

923

Mesmer, a Viennese physician who conducted psychic experiments.

924

Nicot, a French diplomat who first introduced the use of tobacco into France.

925

Pasteur, a French scientist famous for his work in bacteriology.

926

Poinsett, an American statesman and amateur botanist.

927

Pompadour, a favorite of Louis XV of France.

928

Quisling, a Norwegian who collaborated with the Nazis during the Second World War.

929

Rabelais, a French writer of the fifteenth century celebrated for his satire.

930

Sax, a Belgian to whom almost every jazz band is indebted.

931

Solomon, a king in the Old Testament who had several hundred wives.

932

Solon, an Athenian statesman, one of the Seven Wise Men of Greece.

933

Stentor, a Greek herald in the Trojan War described in Homer's *Iliad* as having a powerful voice.

934

Thespis, a Hellenic dramatist credited by tradition with having originated Greek tragedy

935

Titian, an Italian painter whose canvases are notable for a particular color.

936

Volta, an Italian physicist who pioneered in the study of electricity.

937

Words from the Names of Places

The names of many places—towns, cities, provinces, countries, etc.—have entered into the English language as words for other things. Usually, but not always, there is no alteration in spelling, except that the word, unlike the place name, rarely begins with a capital letter. Thus, the word *china* is derived from *China,* from which country fine porcelain was first imported. But occasionally the transformation of a place name into a word does not follow this precise pattern. The word *Percheron,* for instance, which designates a breed of draft horses, stems from *Le Perch,* a district in France where such horses were originally bred.

In the exercises that follow, the name of a place is italicized and accompanied by a statement which identifies the place. On the line below, write the word derived from the place name and a brief definition of the word, as has already been done with the first example. Here, again, use the dictionary whenever you wish.

Academe, the shaded tract of ground near Athens where Plato taught.
academy—a school or an association for promoting learning. 938

Angora, the former name of the capital of Turkey.
939

Arras, a manufacturing and trading town in France.
940

Babel, the Biblical city whose inhabitants tried to build a tower that would reach heaven.
941

Badminton, the name of an estate of an English duke.
942

Bantam, a province in Java.
943

Baux, a town in southeastern France.
944

Bayonne, a French city near the Bay of Biscay.
945

Bikini, the Pacific island where atomic bombs were tested in 1946.
946

Billingsgate, a fish market in London.
947

Bologna, a city in the north of Italy.
948

Buncombe, a county in North Carolina.
949

Calicut, a city in southern India.
950

Cambrai, a textile center in northern France.
951

Cantalupo, a former papal estate near Rome.
952

Cashmere, a state in the north of India.
953

Champagne, the name of a former province in France.
954

Cologne, a major river port on the Rhine in northwestern Germany.

955

Cordova, a city in southern Spain famous for its leather crafts.

956

Fez, a city in Morocco and one of the sacred cities of Islam.

957

Frankfurt, the city in Germany where Goethe was born.

958

Gascony, the region in southern France from which D'Artagnan of *The Three Musketeers* came.

959

Hackney, one of the boroughs of London.

960

Hamburg, the largest German seaport.

961

Havana, the capital of a Caribbean country.

962

Jodhpur, a state in northwestern India.

963

La Grande Chartreuse, a Carthusian monastery in France.

964

Limerick, a county in southern Ireland.

965

Limousin, a region in central France.

966

Lyceum, the grove near Athens where Aristotle discoursed to his students.

967

Magnesia, a region in Greece.

968

Manila, the capital of the Philippines.

969

Marathon, the place from which an Athenian runner set forth with the news that the Persians had been defeated.

970

Meander, the former name of a river in Asia Minor.

971

Mecca, the birthplace of Mohammed.

972

Morocco, a country in North Africa.

973

Palatium, one of the seven hills of Rome where the first Roman emperor lived.

974

Peking, the capital of the Chinese People's Republic.

975

Podunk, a town in Massachusetts.

976

Sardinia, an island in the Mediterranean.

977

Shanghai, the largest city in China.

978

Shillelagh, a village in Ireland.

979

Spa, a town in Belgium, famous for its mineral springs and baths.

980

Sparta, the most warlike of the ancient Greek city-states.

981

Sybaris, an ancient city in Italy famous for its luxury.

982

Tangier, a seaport in Morocco (sometimes spelled *Tanger*).

983

Taranto, a seaport and naval base on the heel of Italy.

984

Waterloo, a Belgian village in the vicinity of which Napoleon met his final defeat.

985

Words from the Names of Characters in Fiction

The names of a number of fictional characters have become words. In Gilbert and Sullivan's opera *The Mikado*, for instance, a character named Pooh-Bah holds many different offices simultaneously. This name became the word *pooh-bah*, which specifies any individual who holds a number of offices at the same time, or simply a person who holds a high office.

More often than not, the names of fictional characters have become words with no change in their spelling, but some have been altered, usually by the addition of a grammatical ending. Similarly, some of them still begin with a capital letter after they have become words, and some do not.

These exercises provide you with the names of fictional characters and information concerning the literary works from which they originated. On the line below each name and the information that accompanies it, write the word to which the name has given rise and a short definition of the word. This has already been done with the first example. You will find it necessary to use the dictionary frequently.

Babbitt, the chief character in the novel of the same name by Sinclair Lewis.

Babbitt—an altogether conventional businessman. 986

Braggadocio, a character in Edmund Spenser's long poem *The Faerie Queene*.

987

Brobdingnagian, an inhabitant of a land of giants in Jonathan Swift's *Gulliver's Travels*.

988

Don Juan, a legendary figure in Spanish folklore who appears as the hero in a number of literary works.

989

Falstaff, a knight in Shakespeare's play *King Henry IV*.

990

Frankenstein, a medical student given to fearful experiments in a novel of the same name by Mary Shelley.

991

Friday, the faithful servant in Daniel Defoe's novel *Robinson Crusoe*.

992

Gargantua, the main character in Rabelais' famous satire *Gargantua and Pantagruel*.

993

Mrs. Grundy, a censorious woman referred to in Thomas Morton's comedy *Speed the Plow*.

994

Lilliputian, a member of a tiny race in Jonathan Swift's *Gulliver's Travels*.

995

Lothario, a young libertine in Nicholas Rowe's play *The Fair Penitent*.

996

Mrs. Malaprop, a woman in Richard Sheridan's play *The Rivals*.

997

Milquetoast, the chief character in a once-popular comic strip created by H. T. Webster.

998

Pandarus, a go-between in love affairs who appears in works by such writers as Chaucer and Shakespeare.

999

page 171

Pantalone, a character who appears in many old Italian comedies and in modern pantomime drama.

1000

Pecksniff, an unattractive character in Charles Dickens' novel *Martin Chuzzlewit.*

1001

Pickwick, the hero of Charles Dickens' novel *Pickwick Papers.*

1002

Pollyanna, the heroine of a novel of the same name by Eleanor Porter.

1003

Quixote, the hero of Cervantes' celebrated novel *Don Quixote.*

1004

Robot, one of the manufactured creatures in the play *R.U.R.* by Karel Capek, the Czech dramatist.

1005

Rodomonte, a character in *Orlando Furioso,* a poem by the Italian author Lodovico Ariosto.

1006

Scrooge, the principal figure in Charles Dickens' story *A Christmas Carol.*

1007

Simon Pure, a character in Susanna Centlivre's play *A Bold Stroke for a Wife.*

1008

Yahoo, a member of a group of vicious and disgusting creatures in Jonathan Swift's *Gulliver's Travels.*

1009

Words from the Names of Mythological Characters

One of the many contributions of classical Greece and Rome to our language consists of English words derived from the names of Greek and Roman gods and goddesses. Thus, the name of the Roman goddess of agriculture, Ceres, gave rise to the English word *cereal*. Occasionally, the name of a classical deity has become, or has formed the basis of, more than one English word. The father of Ceres was Saturn, also associated with agriculture, and his name is the origin for such words as *Saturn* (the planet), *saturnine*, and *saturnalia*.

In the process of becoming a word, the name of a Greek or Roman deity has often been altered, usually by the addition of a grammatical ending, as in *cereal*, *saturnine*, and *saturnalia*. But in other instances, such a name has become a word with no change whatever, except that the word seldom begins with a capital letter.

In these exercises, the name of a classical deity is italicized and followed by a statement that identifies it. On the line below, write a word derived from the name and a brief definition of the word, as has already been done with the first example. Here, too, use the dictionary freely.

Atlas, a Greek god who held up the heavens.

atlas—a book of maps.   1010

Bacchus, the Greek god of wine and festivity.
_____ 1011

Eros, the Greek god of love.
_____ 1012

Fauna, sister of the Roman god Faunus.
_____ 1013

Faunus, the Roman god of animals.
_____ 1014

Flora, the Roman goddess of flowers.
_____ 1015

Hercules, a Greek god of great strength and courage who performed twelve difficult and dangerous tasks.
_____ 1016

Janus, a two-faced Roman god.
_____ 1017

Jove, the Roman god who ruled all the other gods.
_____ 1018

Juno, the goddess of marriage and the wife of Jove.
_____ 1019

Mars, the Roman god of war.
_____ 1020

Mercury, a Roman god usually envisioned as wearing a winged hat and winged sandals.
_____ 1021

Muse, any one of the nine Greek goddesses who presided over the arts and sciences.
_____ 1022

Nemesis, the Greek goddess of retribution whom wrongdoers are supposed eventually to meet.
_____ 1023

Pan, a Greek god with the legs of a goat, patron of shepherds and hunters.
_____ 1024

Pluto, the Greek god who ruled Hades.

1025
_____

Proteus, a Greek sea-god who could change himself into any shape he wished.

1026
_____

Psyche, a princess in Greek mythology who became immortal and the personification of the soul.

1027
_____

Tantalus, a son of Zeus condemned to stand in water up to his chin with branches of fruit just out of reach.

1028
_____

Titan, any one of twelve brothers and sisters in Greek myth, all of whom were giants.

1029
_____

Uranus, the Greek sky-god.

1030
_____

Vulcan, the Roman god of fire and metal-working.

1031
_____